This book is dedicated to all the deal makers
who create millions of jobs by winning deals.
They are the hidden heroes that keep our
economies running.

Praise for Secrets of Sales Innovators

"Jan has, in his book, been able to pinpoint the key success factors in closing large and complex sales pursuits. Closing large deals does not need to be rocket science, but it will require the right set of information, skills and grit. In this book you will find everything you need to have in place to start catching the big fish."

-Martin Evers, CEO, Thurne Teknik Ab

"Secrets of Sales Innovators is a practical guide for making sure you win big deals."

-Harry Nyström, Managing Director, Canon Oy

"Every sales team wants to close bigger and bigger deals. In Secrets of Sales Innovators Jan creates a clear framework for doing so and backs it up with data and interviews from teams that have been truly successful."

-Baman Motivala, VP ISV Sales EMEA & APAC, Salesforce.com

"I'm particularly keen on Jan's idea of creating a mutual action plan with our customer, particularly when we base it on working backwards from the customer's desired outcomes. This concept, as well as many others in Jan's new book, should be adopted by any serious sales organization."

-**Bob Apollo, Founder of Inflexion-Point** - the Outcome-Centric Selling experts

"Winning large and complex deals is essential for any direct sales force to be successful, because changes in client behavior is driving smaller deals to alternative sales channels. Secrets of Sales Innovators by Jan Ropponen is an excellent step-by-step reference guide to help you win more large deals."

-**Jan Aalto, Sales Operations Director NA Sending Technology Solutions, Pitney Bowes Inc.**

"Our sales team has worked together with Jan to build a more structured way of winning bigger deals. In his book he shares great ideas and insights on what it takes for modern sales professionals to consistently win larger deals"

-**Stefan Kristjansson, Head of Sales Denmark and Sweden, F-Secure**

"I have been in sales for 20+ years in different roles; as a sales consultant, account executive and in sales management. Jan's book is a great read and shows with some solid facts that large complex sales cycles require you to engage early, have a plan and vision for your deal, and manage the right level of engagements with the relevant customer stakeholders. This is an excellent book for both starters and senior sellers."

-Sven Heijnen, VP Sales EMEA Comms & Media at Vlocity

"Each deal is different and while you can follow blueprints to success, it does take innovation and investing strategic thought in each account to push your company/product over the edge. Jan's book has some great ideas on how to make this happen."

-Jim Rahill, Regional VP of Sales, Tradeshift

"Sales theory, practice and results are three elements that Jan thoughtfully explores, relating valuable personal experiences that can be applied to devastating effect. Collectively, the contributors have made their impossible dreams a reality, and Jan has brought their stories together for others to learn from. This is a must read for anyone seeking to smash it in sales."

-Matthew Lockwood, Director of Strategic Accounts at Dixa

Contact publisher:
Jan Ropponen
jan@janropponen.com

ISBN 978-952-69079-5-6 (paperback)
ISBN 978-952-69079-6-3 (eBook)

Bulk discounts available. Contact publisher for details.

Table of contents

Introduction

How Do the Best Sellers Consistently Win Big Deals?

Gaining the experience to consistently close six-figure deals can take decades. As an educator in the field, it's a topic I often discuss with sales leaders and their teams. Based on these discussions, I began documenting the habits of world-class deal makers—specifically, what makes them successful. This was the catalyst for starting this research project, the result of which are right here in this book. My purpose was to simplify the how, what, when, and where of the best of the best so you, too, can close career-changing deals.

This book is for anyone who wants to step up their sales game. If you're looking to consistently win deals worth $100,000 or more, the knowledge curated within these pages will help you do just that. Whether you're working on deals yourself or coaching others to win them, this book is your quick reference guide to success.

Top-performers with ten or more years experience (who consistently make President's Club) are represented within this book. They've shared their most valuable lessons throughout their careers to help accelerate your learning curve. The content is structured around easy to use tips and tricks to move any major deal forward.

One deal at a time, the knowledge in this book will guide you to be a more consistent sales performer. I guarantee it!

Jan Ropponen

Terminology

Deal Maker - Throughout the book the phrase "deal maker" is used to describe the sales professionals referred to in the following pages.

Prospect - In the first stage of the sales process (Identify), the term "prospect" is used to describe the customer (or potential new customer). The deals analyzed in the research include both prospects and existing customers.

Prospecting – An activity that leads to identifying and creating new opportunities

Stakeholder - A person on the customer's side who in one way or another is involved in (or linked to) a purchase decision

Opportunity - A potential deal that's been qualified

Discovery - A series of interviews, meetings or workshops that uncover information to help the deal maker (and the customer) understand problems better in order to find the best solution

RFI - Request for information (sent before RFP)

RFP - Request for proposal. Some may use the term RFQ, referring to quotes, but this is typically only used for smaller transactions.

Quick Guide

III - POSITION

IV - CLOSE

Chapter 1

What it takes to succeed?

What's changed?

Extremely independent customers

Professional procurement

Customers have more options

More stakeholders involved in deals

Decisionmakers are tough to reach

Commoditization (competing products seem the same to customers)

Price transparency

Decision making has moved up in organizations

These changes lead to:

- Longer sales cycles
- Margin pressure
- Lower win-rates

*Answers based on the interview question:
"What changes have you observed in the last 15-20 years?"

3 Skills Deal Makers Need to Master

The requirements for sales professionals in the 21st century are more demanding than ever before because sales professionals must act as change agents if they want to win large, complex deals. The following are three crucial skills to master in order to succeed in today's economy:

Business Acumen – Learning to understand business logic, market trends, business models, financials, and strategy are key.

Domain Expertise – Using valuable insights within a particular business process or field adds value to customers. One example of domain expertise could be "supply chain management."

Consultative Skills – The ability to discuss options and how they impact the customer's financial performance is necessary in guiding them to a final decision.

Notes

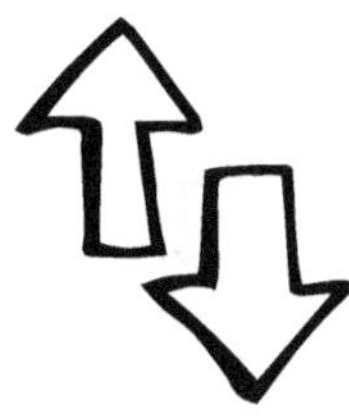

Chapter 2

The Difference Between Winning and Losing a Deal

Key Differences Between Won and Lost Deals

The graphic below shows the variables that were present in the won deals that were analyzed in the research. In lost deals these variables were not addressed properly or sometimes even missing completely. When done properly, both collaboration and consultation create value and differentiate the best deal makers and their teams from competitors. With improved collaboration, the chances of effective consultative selling go up exponentially. The more you are able to create business value through consultation, the more willing the customer is to collaborate. It's hard to succeed in one area without the other. The remainder of the book focuses on how to succeed in covering the variables below in order to increase the probability of closing career-changing deals.

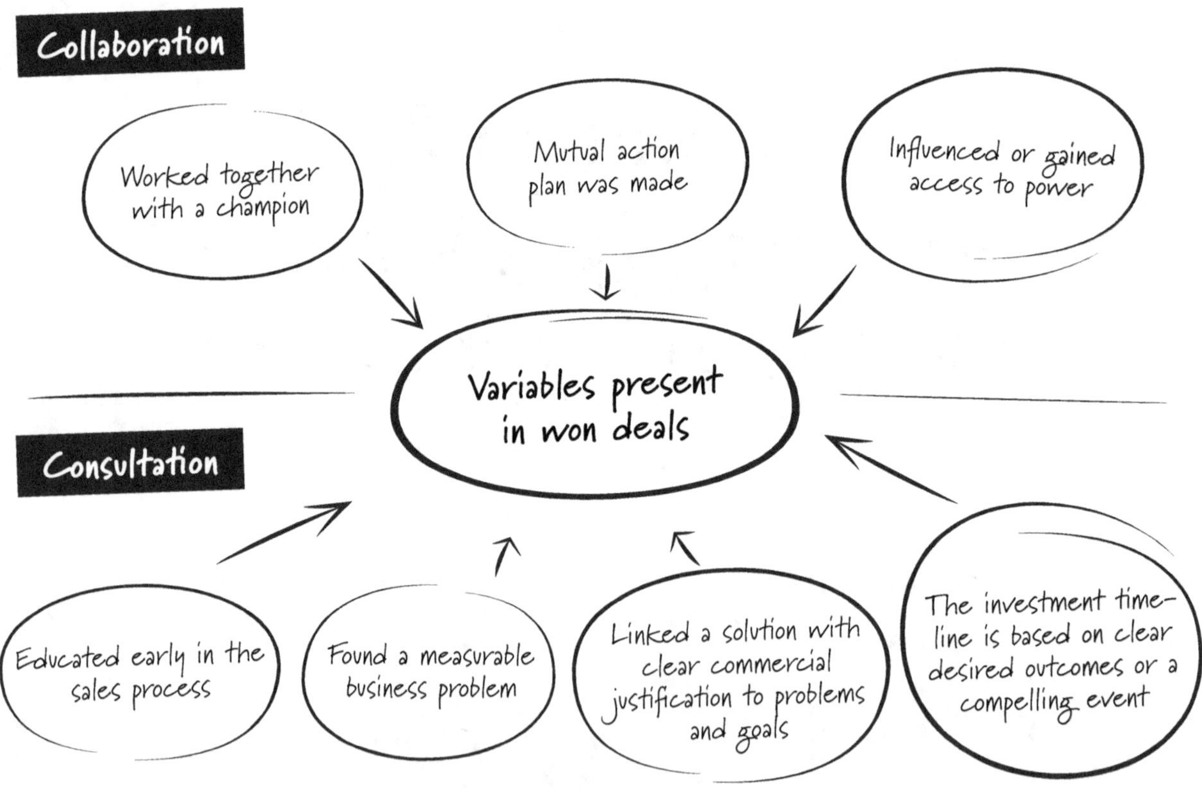

Creating Value on Two Levels

Tips from Deal Makers

Creating Value Through Collaboration

» Adjust your sales approach to match the unique situations of important stakeholders

» Co-create the right solution with the customer

» Build relationships with champions and other allies early and work together with them

» Gain credibility with C-Level execs by collaborating with stakeholders below them

» Connect your own team members and experts with the right stakeholders

» Involve the client in all stages and communicate consistently

» Facilitate the customer's buying process by making things easier for them

"If they are not collaborating with you then they are collaborating with somebody else."

Tips from Deal Makers

Creating value by consulting

- » Understand the customer's business situation as well as the perspectives of different stakeholders and their problems

- » Educate the customer in every meeting

- » Focus on the customer's desired business outcomes, not products and features

- » Add value to the customer's understanding of their problems and options

- » Be professional when challenging a customer's thinking and ideas

- » Clearly communicate the commercial benefits of your solution, linking it to their strategy

"Customers want to work with vendors that can teach them."

Winning vs Losing

During the interview process, deal makers were asked how
likely they were to win a deal in specific situations.
Turn the page for helpful quotes and statistics!

What are your chances of winning a deal you pursue if you **receive the RFP** from a company you have not been engaged with earlier?

29%

What are your chances of winning an opportunity if **you are the one who created the need to buy** for the customer?

80%

Interview comments

*"Someone is most often helping the customer create RFP's.
If it's not you, then someone else will be in pole position for the win."*

*"You must choose carefully which deals you want to win and go all-in on them,
because being early and working proactively is very resource intensive,
but it's a must if you want to increase your chances of winning."*

*"Unless I have a clear advantage over others, I will never participate
in an RFP, especially if I haven't been involved early."*

ENGAGING EARLY IS CRUCIAL FOR WINNING DEALS!

> What are your chances of winning a deal if you
> do not **meet the final decision maker?**
>
> # 41%

Interview comments

"At some stage you have to be able to get the point of view of the final decision-maker. It doesn't have to be at the beginning but you must earn the access to meet with them if you want to win."

"Only if I have a strong champion on my side do I have a chance to win a deal even if I don't personally connect with the final decision-maker."

GAINING ACCESS TO STAKEHOLDERS HIGHER IN THE ORGANIZATION SUBSTANTIALLY INCREASES WIN-RATES!

If the customer does not want to **collaborate,**
what are your chances of winning?

26%

Interview comments

"The differences and nuances in technology options are really thin. Ultimately most deals come down to, do they trust me to deliver on my word. When things go wrong, as they often do, will I be a person they can call to help fix it? Without deep collaboration, there is no trust."

"Without a champion or sponsor to work with we will always be working reactively and can't lead the deal forward."

COLLABORATION IS ESSENTIAL TO BUILD TRUST AND CREATE A WINNING VALUE PROPOSITION!

Chapter 3

Buying Stages and The Window of Influence

Typical Buying Stages in Complex Deals

Here are typical buying stages with examples of customer-actions in each stage. After this, we'll look at how the deal making process fits with this buying process and where deal makers start their sales process in order to increase the chances of winning the sale.

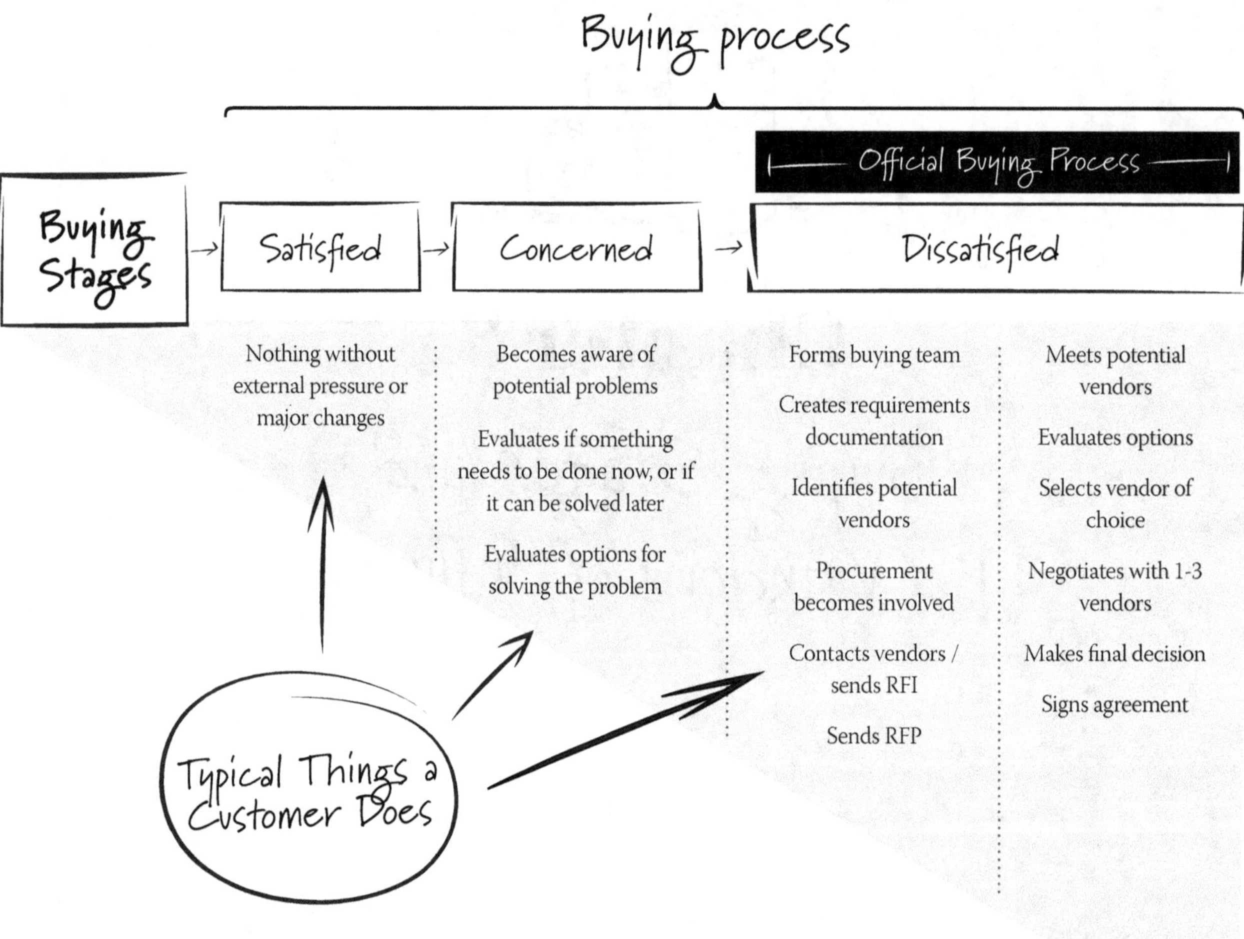

Fitting the Buying and Selling Processes Together

The official sales process of the companies world-class deal makers work for typically have 5-8 key stages. After analyzing these stages, 4 essential phases emerged.

The goal of each stage in the sales process is to proactively move the customer along in their buying process one step at a time, ultimately positioning your solution (and yourself) as a vendor that uniquely fits their needs.

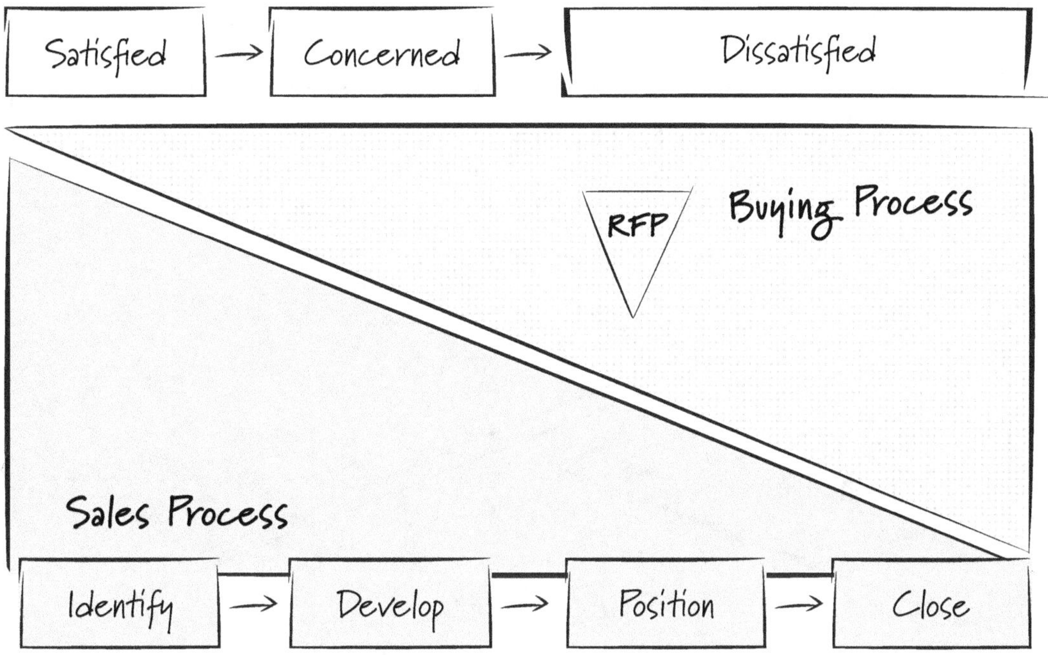

Engaging in the right stage of the customer's buying process is crucial. If you want to increase your chances of winning, focus on engaging with the customer in the Window of Influence.

Deal makers who get involved late in the buying process have a difficult time influencing the customer, which decreases their chances of winning.

It's clear that the best deal makers invest a majority of their time in the first half of the sales process. If they're unable to engage early, they do their best to get the customer to reconsider what their requirements should be, which means pausing for a moment or even moving the customer backwards in their buying process.

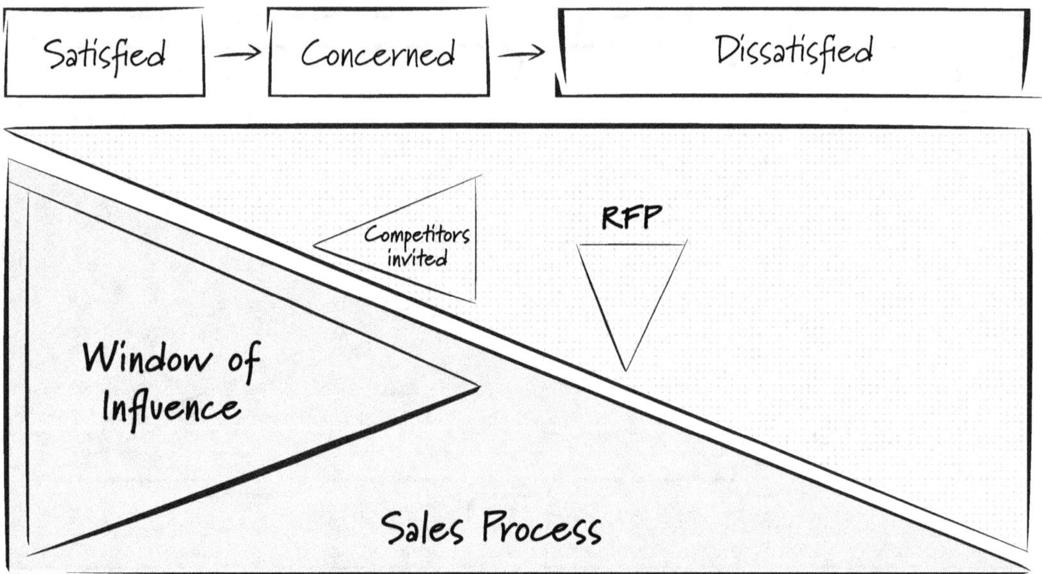

The Later You Engage, the Lower the Probability of Winning Becomes

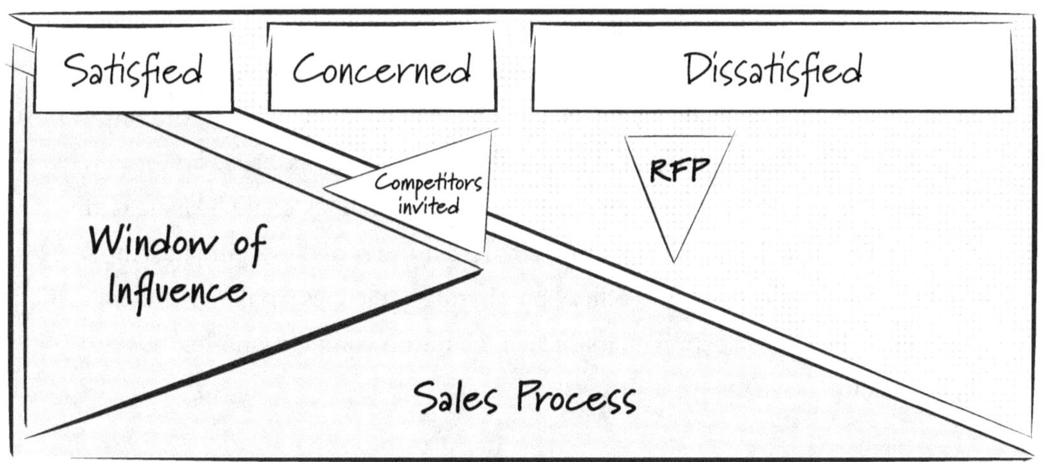

Chances of winning if you craft a vision and help the customer create their plans

74%[1]

Chances of winning when responding to customer requests

26%[1]

RFP win-rates are much lower

"5% is the standard win-rate on RFP's"[2]

Average RFP win-rates can in some industries be between 5-15%, while average win-rates are between 25-35% (based on my experience)

Shaping the RFP
Before the Competition

"Anthony" was able to leverage the network of an executive in his company in order to secure a meeting with a C-level stakeholder at a manufacturing company. The manufacturer had major challenges with the profitability of several of their plants and Anthony believed he could help boost their profitability with a service concept they had in their portfolio. The C-level stakeholder gave Anthony permission to audit the performance metrics of several plants, because Anthony promised he would create an assessment of how profitability could be increased. At this point there were no competitors in the game. From the beginning, Anthony knew that the prospect's official purchasing guidelines would force them to place the vendor selection up for bid, which meant competition—but no one but Anthony was in the game just yet!

Based on Anthony's team's audit, a realistic assessment of the prospect's problems was created, along with a list of recommendations. While the audit was in progress, the customer put together a project team responsible for choosing the right vendor. The team leader of the project team let Anthony know that they would also invite three other competitors. The competitors had not engaged with the C-level as Anthony had and were going to have to answer the RFP that Anthony's team were doing their best to influence. Several weeks after the competitors were invited, the official RFP was sent out.

Anthony knew he had an excellent chance of winning the deal, because several elements in the RFP were almost identical to the documentation he had provided, such as the vendors responsibilities, how the costs should be divided up, the penalty fees, and the contract period. In essence, a majority of the RFP was shaped based on the audit and the best practices that Anthony's team had shared.

Anthony was able to build a good relationship with the team leader of the buyer's team, even though their goal was to rattle and pressure Anthony to get the best deal. The plans of implementing Anthonys service, which was a part of the RFP, were presented to the whole project team and C-level, as well as one-on-one meetings with plant managers (who would be very involved when the service concept was implemented). Anthonys team had already met most of the plant managers during the audit and knew their buy-in and trust were crucial for the project team.

In the end, it was clear that the customer wanted to work with Anthony's team. During negotiations, Anthony and his team received a tip about competitor service costs, helping to ensure Anthony's solution was chosen. After weeks of negotiations, Anthony and his team were able to close the deal and start helping the customer.

Lessons Learned

The customer wanted to buy from Anthony because several important stakeholders believed in their plan, which included realistic data and diagnostics from Anthony's team's initial audit. Anthony put himself in a good position to win profitably because he was able to influence early in the process through collaboration, making it easier to position himself as the best overall option.

Value Creation Happens Early

When you succeed in the "window of influence," it's easier to compete in later sales stages. In the early stages, you are co-creating together with the customer. When done correctly, it will make your offering unique and hard to compare with others. During what is a rather limited *window of influence*, the deal maker focuses on provoking with insights and showing possibilities without focusing on the product or service they sell. The seller, through their experience and knowledge becomes part of the solutions value in the eyes of the customer. This book shows how differentiation is done during the *window of influence*.

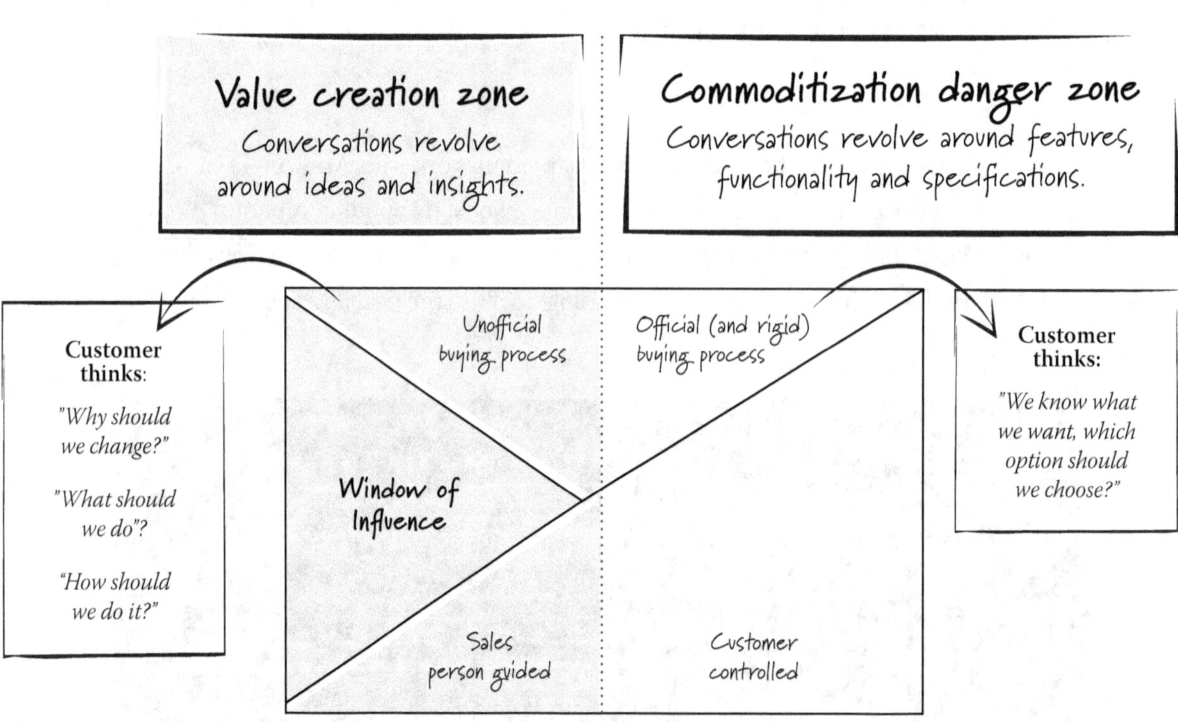

The book is split into the four sales stages, each represented by it's own part. The stages form a flexible framework that functions as a guideline for winning larger deals. This is an ideal sequence of events for deal makers to follow in order to close deals, but we have to acknowledge the reality that the sales process often starts from an RFP or a lead, at which point, closing becomes a question of how well the deal maker can engage with the customer. This often means moving back and forth between stages, even simultanous completion of several stages as needed. At the end of the book, you'll find a checklist of all the main ideas from the different stages as a quick reference guide for winning large deals.

Notes

....

....

....

....

....

....

....

The first two stages have one goal: Moving the customer forward. Based on data from successful deals worth $100,000 or more, the number of customer meetings from start to finish are anywhere between 5-50+ depending on the size of the deal, as well as factors like who you are selling to (prospects versus existing customers), and/or the client's overall familiarity with what you are specifically selling.

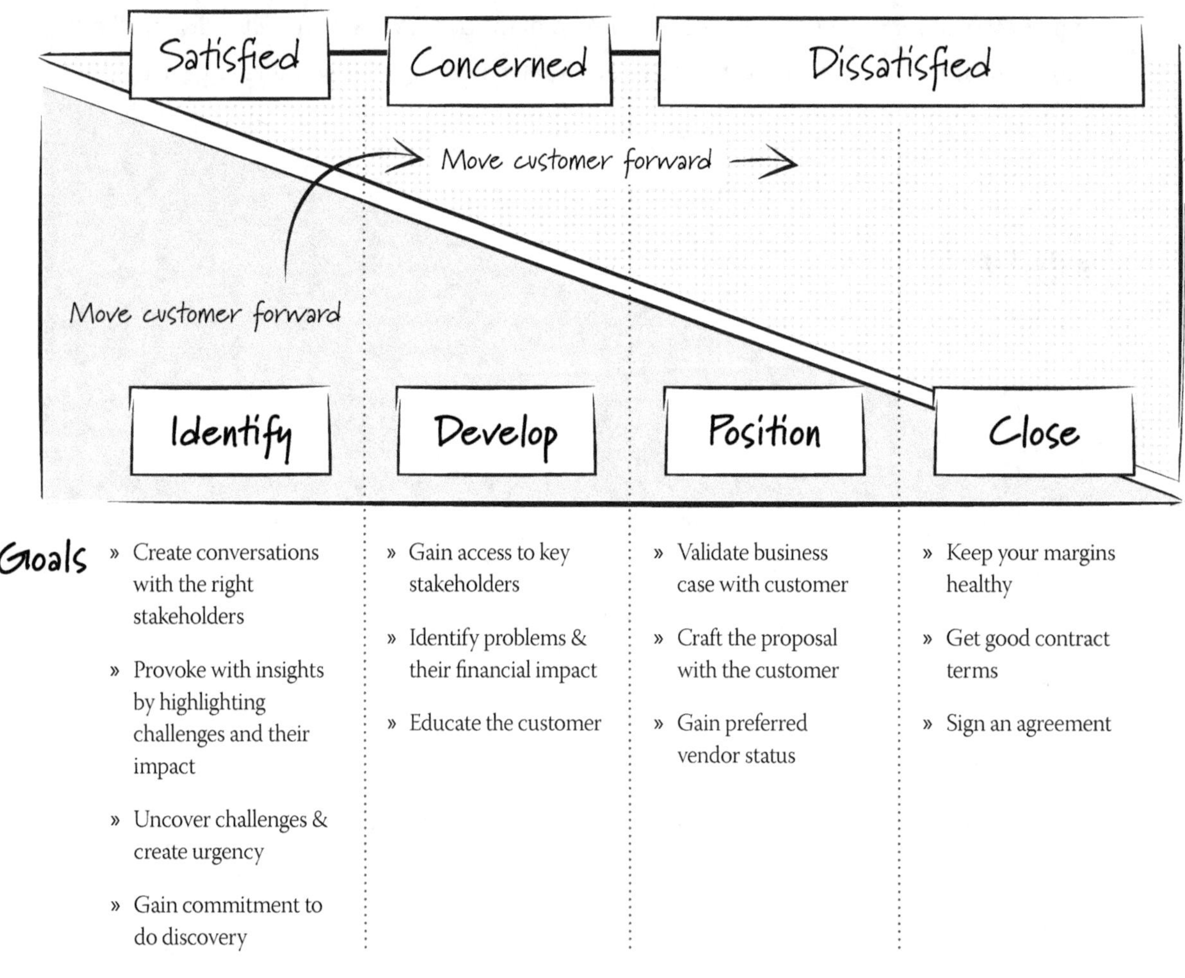

Goals	» Create conversations with the right stakeholders	» Gain access to key stakeholders	» Validate business case with customer	» Keep your margins healthy
	» Provoke with insights by highlighting challenges and their impact	» Identify problems & their financial impact	» Craft the proposal with the customer	» Get good contract terms
	» Uncover challenges & create urgency	» Educate the customer	» Gain preferred vendor status	» Sign an agreement
	» Gain commitment to do discovery			

Summary of Winning vs. Losing

In the highly competitive business environment that 21st century companies now operate in, winning deals comes down to having a differentiated sales approach. Closing six and seven-figure deals requires creating more value at earlier stages in the buying process than your competitors.

The best deal makers create an excess of value and build trust to the extent that they become an inextricable part of the solution's overall value in the eyes of the customer.

Notes

PART I
Identifying Opportunities

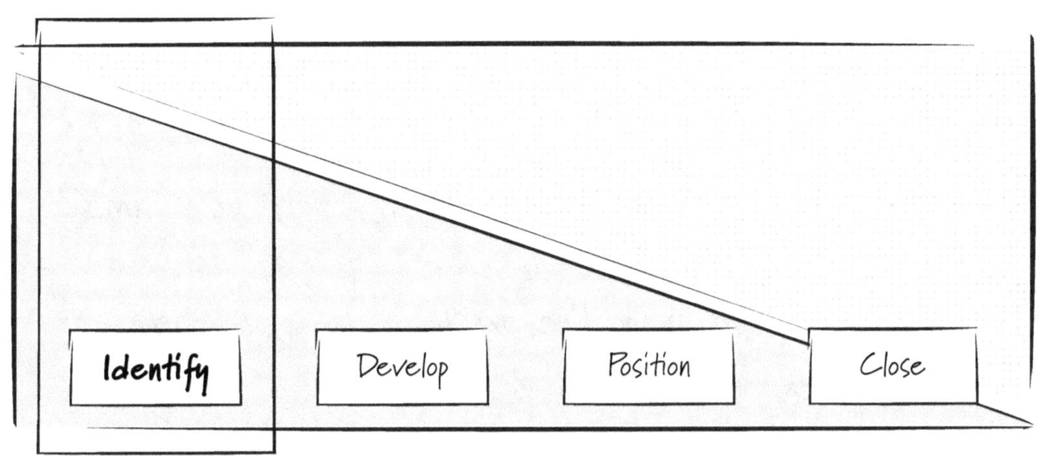

The Goals of This Stage

Create conversations and interest with the right stakeholders by using insights and ideas

Uncover challenges you can help create solutions for

Validate the opportunity itself—is it worth your time?

Gain commitment from the prospect to spend time and resources on discovery

Evaluate Your Deal Making Habits

How are you creating value for the prospect in the beginning of your sales process?

What is your way of differentiating yourself and building trust in the first meetings and calls?

Is your sales approach in the first meeting always based on the buyers unique situation?

Do you properly justify why the prospect should spend time with you to do discovery?

Notes

Chapter 4

Prospecting

"A lot of sales people fail because they are too busy foolishly going after all kinds of business."

Maintain a Constant Flow of Opportunities

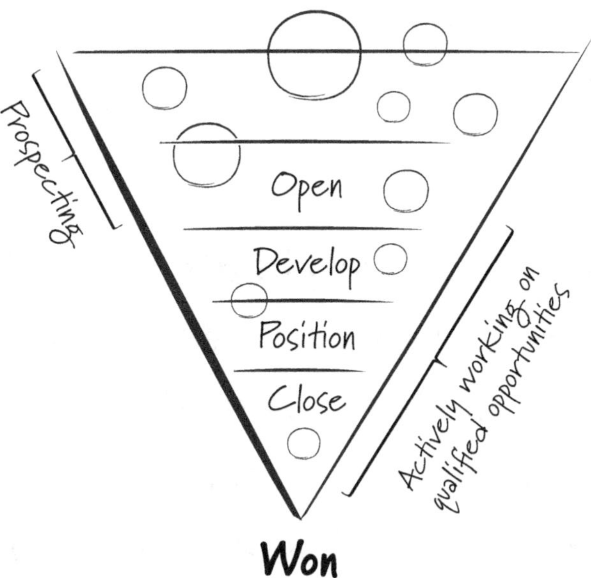

World-class deal makers are adept at qualification, or, knowing which opportunities to pursue. Top deal makers close big deals because they are very selective on where they focus their time, energy and resources.

"Qualify carefully and once you commit, go all in."

The best of the best are not afraid to decline or skip an opportunity they don't think is worth pursuing. The competitive market requires being more deliberate; it's hard to win deals you can't fully focus on, especially if you're unable to utilize internal resources to help win the deal. That just equates to a big waste of time. The interviews revealed that successful deal makers have learned to avoid being overly opportunistic and instead, focus on the right type of accounts in the right industries.

"I never want to overestimate my ability to win, because there are so many deal factors we cannot impact. Even if my team and I do everything right on some opportunities, there is a high chance we will still lose. If I want to win, we really have to focus on finding and developing the right opportunities."

Continuous Prospecting is Key

Without a robust pipeline, sales professionals can get desperate and end up focusing on low quality opportunities. This puts you in the position of trying to force customers to buy what they're not yet ready to buy. For this reason, the best deal makers advise to continuously prospect through the use of as many early stage discussions as possible, both with prospects and existing customers. This way, you're more likely to be in a position of power, giving yourself the ability to choose which opportunities to pursue.

"Taking long-view is difficult because selling is very much about filling a short-term need. You're always going to have pressure from your managers about doing your numbers, but ultimately (that focus) will negatively impact your results—whether trying to close a deal when funding isn't there, or forcing a deal to close even though it doesn't sit with the customer's timeline."

"Your prospects have 13 hours of stuff to do in an 8-hour workday, so whatever you want to talk to them about has to be highly relevant."

Engaging the Right Stakeholders

Just like individuals, companies have a countless amount of problems that often remain unsolved. Even though some employees feel that the problems should be solved, there is a constant battle for how budgets are used. Even though there are on average 10.1[1] people involved in decision making, only one or two stakeholders may be ready to risk their reputation and careers in order to sponsor and support a bigger purchase. These stakeholder are typically in higher positions of power within the organization. The stakeholders that have the biggest incentive and gain the most from your product or services being implemented and have political power, are the ones you should be going after in the beginning. Identifying who this is may be very hard, but deal makers figure out who this could be and then partner up with them.

Getting to power as early as possible, is something deal makers want to achieve. Getting stuck with lower level operational stakeholders slows down deal cycles and makes qualifying whether you have a real opportunity or not very difficult.

"The person who cares the most about what you are selling may be the least able to buy."

"You cannot sell to someone who cannot buy, but you can get information from them to figure out if pursuing the business is worth your while."

Stakeholder Levels

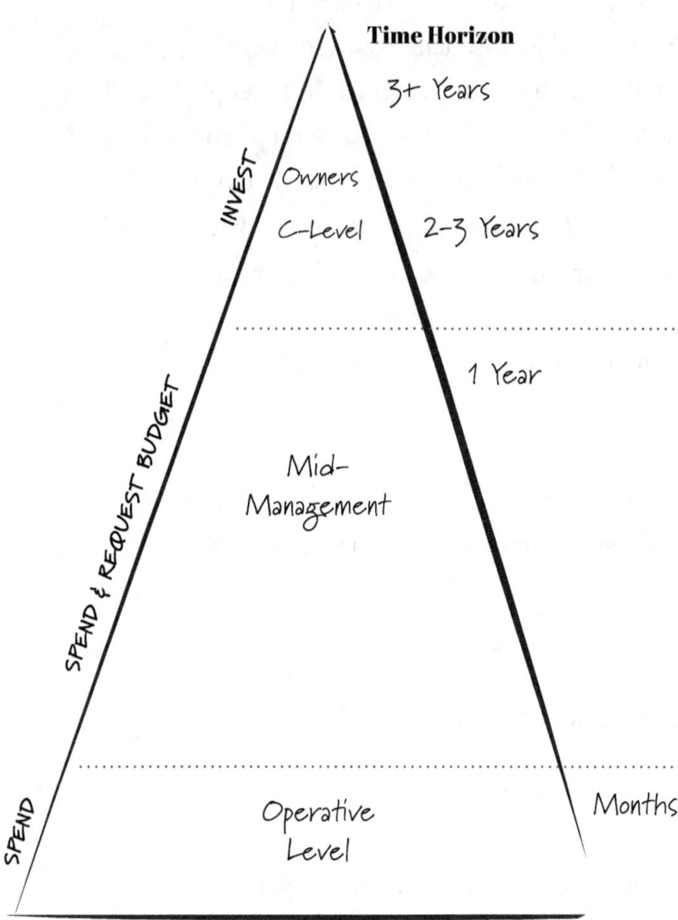

What Drives Each Stakeholder Level

This level is seldomly interested in details. They will invest in strategic matters and business outcomes that lead to increased market share, higher profitability, increased revenue etc.. Since this level has the power over resources, they can move money from one project to another, if they think it's the best for the company. Therefore if they see a new and better idea, they can steal funding from the other projects, to fund their new ideas.

This level is often interested in reaching specific financial goals and metrics set for their division or department. They are mostly interested in the impact of the problems they are experiencing, if they are stopping them from achieving their objectives.

This level is in an important role when budgets are created, and they can often request funding if they have interesting projects.

This level is mostly interested in solving process problems and often interested in features and functionality that make their lives easier.

Operative level employees will typically avoid guiding sellers upwards to power. Caution is needed when working with this level since they typically do not have decision-making power and often lack the relationships with upper management.

Dangers of a Bottom-up Approach

A manager was looking for a new ERP software solution and wanted to meet "Joanna," the account manager of a vendor with a potentially promising solution. The service manager had already looked at videos of their demos and liked what he saw. In the first phone call, the manager said they would soon start the process to, "actively look for a solution."

In the next meeting the manager told Joanna, "I'm responsible for the evaluation, and I've been given the responsibility from our management team to find a solution and make the decision about what solution we should buy." The manager explained how he does not want Joanna to approach anyone else within the organization, especially management because they have given him the responsibility to select the right vendor. Based on Joanna's initial qualification, she could see that this company would benefit from her solution, but it was not as business critical for the industry they operated in, compared to her other customers.

> "I'm responsible for the evaluation, and I've been given the responsibility from our management team to find a solution and make the decision."

Joanna only had one meeting with the prospect because the manager was only interested in features and functions of the technology and didn't want to discuss the business case or have a proper discovery workshop to talk about real business impact. The manager was not able to communicate clearly why and when their challenges needed to be solved. Five years later, Joanna heard that they still didn't have a new solution because they had other priorities at higher levels in the organization.

If the fit had greater potential, Joanna would have figured out a way to get to power. In this case, she thought it wouldn't be worth her time.

Lessons Learned
If management has other priorities that mid or low-level managers are unaware of, the chances of getting funding are often very low. Stakeholders often let salespeople know they have more power than they actually have.

Personal initiatives like this happen all the time. They get pushed up from the bottom in hopes of getting management interested enough that funding could be secured someday.

Approaches for Different Stakeholder Levels

These are not definitive truths, but guidelines for what type of approach is typically needed if you want to engage with a certain stakeholder level in larger organizations. If you are selling to smaller organizations it will be easier to reach upper management with less personalized messaging.

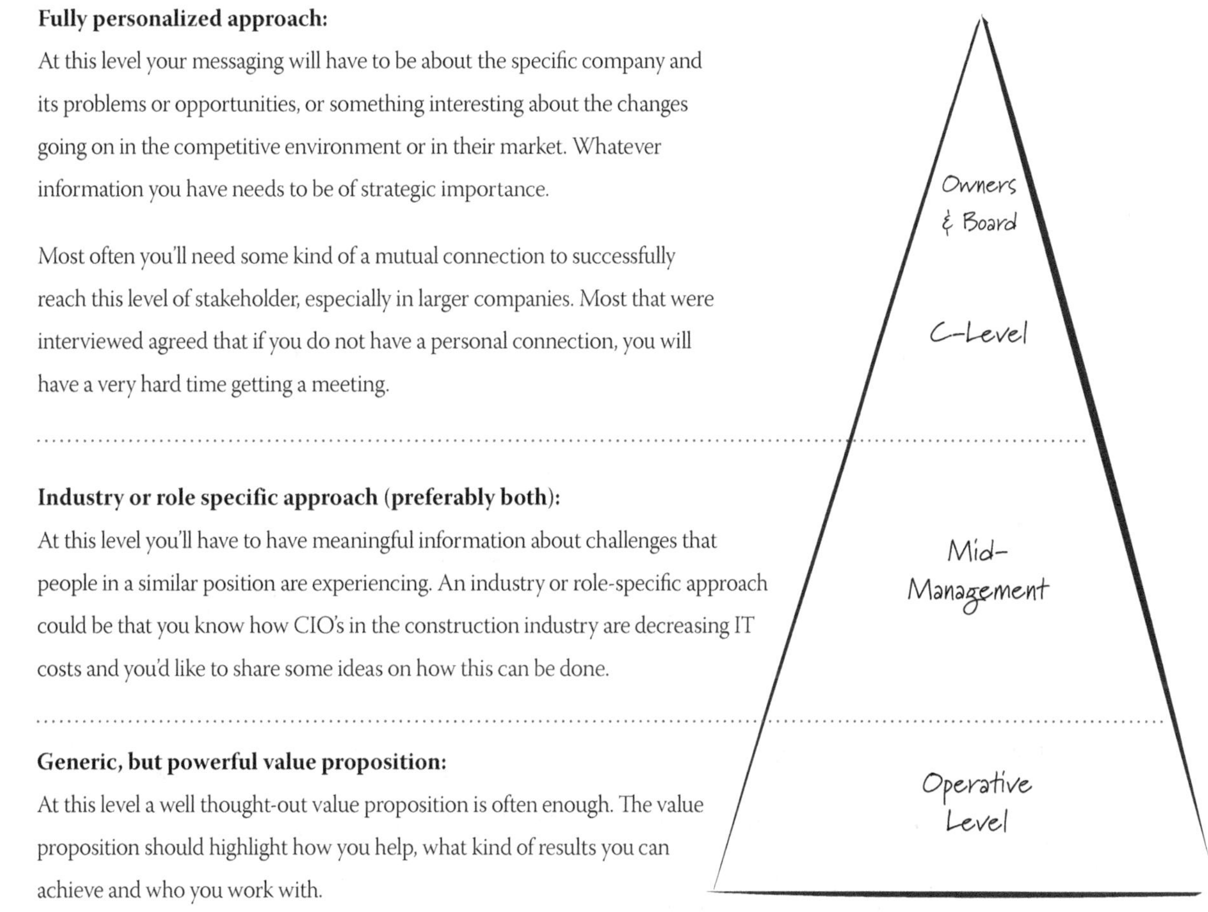

Fully personalized approach:

At this level your messaging will have to be about the specific company and its problems or opportunities, or something interesting about the changes going on in the competitive environment or in their market. Whatever information you have needs to be of strategic importance.

Most often you'll need some kind of a mutual connection to successfully reach this level of stakeholder, especially in larger companies. Most that were interviewed agreed that if you do not have a personal connection, you will have a very hard time getting a meeting.

Industry or role specific approach (preferably both):

At this level you'll have to have meaningful information about challenges that people in a similar position are experiencing. An industry or role-specific approach could be that you know how CIO's in the construction industry are decreasing IT costs and you'd like to share some ideas on how this can be done.

Generic, but powerful value proposition:

At this level a well thought-out value proposition is often enough. The value proposition should highlight how you help, what kind of results you can achieve and who you work with.

Many Paths Can Lead You to the Same Stakeholder

You can either try to reach the right stakeholder directly or use a number of different paths to reach them. Being referred by someone increases the chances of getting a meeting, especially if you know the person referring you very well and they already have a relationship with the stakeholder you want to meet.

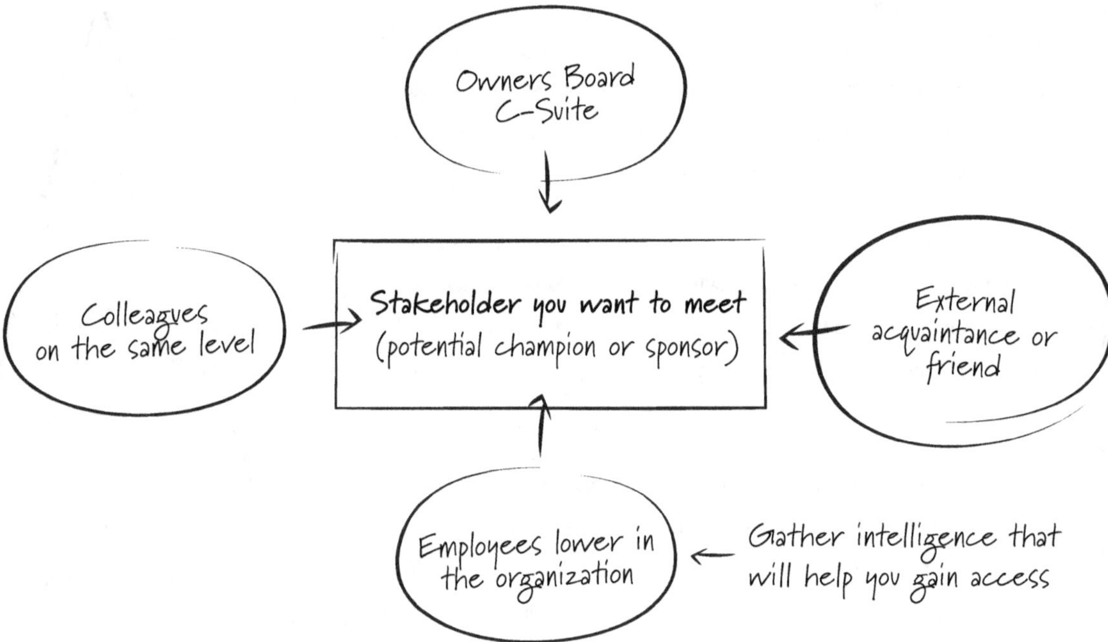

"YOU ARE 4.2X MORE LIKELY TO GET AN APPOINTMENT IF YOU HAVE A PERSONAL CONNECTION WITH A BUYER." [2]

Reaching the C-level Through Your Connections

A new CEO had just been appointed in a prospect account that "Anthony" had been working on for a year. In the past few years Anthony had tried to engage with other executives but he hadn't been able to create enough interest to gain access to them. He was only able to access stakeholders below the executive team.

Now however the company's profitability had decreased for a few years and the newly appointed CEO's main objective was most likely to turn the profitability back on the right path. Anthony had a strong feeling that a service concept his company had could be a good fit for them, now that profitability was a key issue.

An execuitve of the business unit used to be colleagues with the prospects CEO.

It just so happened that an executive in Anthony's business unit used to be the colleague of the newly appointed CEO some years ago.

Once Anthony found out that there was this type of mutual connection between this prospects CEO and a colleague of his, he was able to leverage this relationship to get a meeting.

Before initiating contact with the CEO, Anthony did the necessary background work. The newly appointed CEO had a few critical objectives. Anthony decided what the best references were, and then using the references and the mutual connection to approach the CEO, he was able to get the first meeting. It became apparent very quick to both parties in the first meeting that this was something worth looking into. Less than a year later, they had signed an agreement for a very large, multi-year service agreement.

Lessons Learned

Use the network of others to gain access. Don't be lazy and only use the mutual contact for access. Do your homework, otherwise you are at risk of being delegated to lower levels. Early access to the right level of stakeholders often increases win-rates and deal velocity.

Using Valuable Insights to Gain Access

The higher you want to access, the more insights you'll need. Some deal makers call the ability to use insights and ideas as being a "visionary" sales professional. You need information that will trigger them to want to spend time with you and discuss things in more detail in a formal meeting.

Examples of beneficial background information used to create insights:

- What are the critical factors to succeeding in their industry?
- What are trends or major changes happening in the customer's market?
- What are competitors doing that the prospect is not doing?

For customers that are satisfied with their current situation and not interested in meeting with you, you must be able to provoke their thinking. Many deal makers explain how they leverage data—one way or another—to create relevant insights, which they then use to predict what could potentially happen to the prospect and their business. Successful deal makers use this type of insight to gain access to important stakeholders.

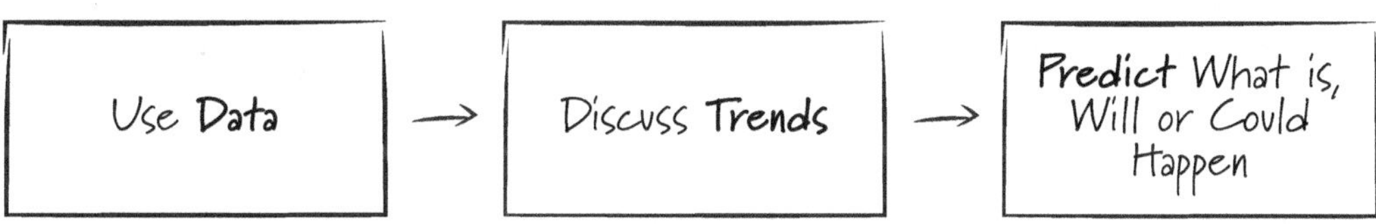

Scaling Prospecting Efforts

Prospecting can be scaled better than ever before with the help of account based marketing (ABM) or business development representatives (BDR). Both of these were things that many deal makers mentioned have made them much more efficient in their prospecting efforts.

BDR Supporting the Deal Maker

Traditionally the deal maker would do all of the prospecting work themselves. Instead of spending valuable time on prospecting, in some instances it makes sense to give a majority of the heavy workload of prospecting to a BDR. This allows the deal maker to fully focus on working on their opportunities in the pipeline. Many of the interviewed deal makers have BDRs supporting them.

Here are examples of how some deal makers (DM) work with BDRs:

1. The DM creates a long-list of potential prospects that are a good fit for what he/she is selling

2. The BDR takes the list and starts working on it by researching the accounts and the different stakeholders within the accounts

3. A short list of 10-30 companies is created once background work has been done

4. The BDR engages the companies and hands over early stage potential opportunities for the DM to start working on

5. For those prospects that are not ready, the BDR creates a follow-up task or hands over to marketing for nurturing

Initial Qualification Before the First Meeting

At this point, when you have initiated contact the first time, the goal is not just to book a meeting. In many situations it makes sense to qualify and understand the prospect's situation before setting up the first meeting in order to avoid wasting time.

The goal is to find out if they are experiencing similar challenges or likely to face similar challenges in the future (similar to previous customers). Are they experiencing pain or are they a very likely to experience pain at some point? If so, it makes sense to book a meeting.

In the prospecting stage do a quick check about these two things before booking a meeting:

1. Fit - Does what they potentially need fit what we do?

2. Power - Do we have access to power or can we work our way to power through the person we are now talking to?

Qualifying Leads

The risk of not being a good fit is higher on inbounds so start qualifying immediately before dedicating resources and time to do proper discovery.

Deal makers advice on the subject is very consistent:

> *"Be careful or at least skeptical of leads, because they are often from companies that may not be an ideal fit."*

Inbounds can often be so called "bottom-up" attempts. This means low level stakeholders just do their own research projects internally for "future" needs or in an effort to educate themselves. In these situations, the deal maker must quickly evaluate whether this lead can generate real business and whether this person could lead them to others within the organization.

 **Things Deal Makers Try to Understand**

1. **Who** - Who in the organization is aware of this person doing research? Are they by themselves or is there a project team? Which department or unit does this impact and will they be funding this purchase?

2. **What** - What are they looking to solve?

3. **When** - When does this problem need to be solved?

4. **Why** - Is there a real business problem that must be solved or would it just be nice to solve? How high on their priority list is this problem?

"On inbounds be very aware of tire kickers doing research projects."

Minimum Tasks for Qualifying Leads

Analyze the following:

What is the customer's buying situation and current criteria?

Is the person that contacted you doing research alone or is there a broader recognition of the needs within the organization?

Are you in a competitive situation?

Based on this analysis, make a rational decision to pursue or not to pursue

Chapter 5

First Meetings

Goals of the First Meeting

1. Gain the customers trust

The customer begins to trust you, because you demonstrate a high level of business acumen, industry & domain expertise.

Your company is seen as credible, because it has helped others with similar challenges before, with great results.

2. Understand the customers needs

You understand what they want to achieve and what stands in their way.

You have diagnosed if the customer has serious enough problems that would warrant a solution.

3. Qualify and decide next steps

You qualify whether moving forward makes sense, based on at least the following criteria:

- When do they want to improve their current state?

- Will the customer commit resources and time to do discovery?

- Who needs to be involved & who will potentially fund the investment?

Preparing Before the Meeting

Building trust and creating value in the first meeting is critical, if you want to earn the right to do discovery and move forward in pursuing the opportunity.

In tough competitive markets and big deals, your first meeting may be the most important one. You may only get one chance to meet a very important stakeholder, so make the most of it.

The larger the potential opportunity, the more of an incentive there is to prepare properly before engaging with the prospect in the first meeting, especially if it's with someone on a higher level in the organization.

Ideas for preparing — find out the following:

What do other sales people in your company know about the industry or this specific prospect? (often colleagues have engaged with similar customers)

What are critical factors to their industry and their competitiveness in the market?

How is their business model changing and what are the their industry's trends?

Who are their competitors?

How is the prospect performing financially and what is their outlook?

What are typical problems this type of company may be experiencing?

What insights could spark their interest?

What are our best references that match this prospect?

"If you are sitting in front of, let's say a retailer, you need to know about Amazon. You need to know about the threats retailers face and what other companies are doing and the costs of doing things the old way in that industry."

"The best way to have valuable insights is to go to events, read periodicals, and involve and engross yourself in the customer's industry. The more experienced I've become, the more I've understood just how important this is. If I'm up against someone who is not as prepared as I am, I'm going to beat them every time."

Preparing Before the Meeting

To be trustworthy and seen as a credible asset, you should be able to lead your conversations with the statements below, and have in depth discussions around the three topics.

If you have prepared properly, you can have strategically significant conversations that prospects/customers appreciate. The key is to have a point of view in advance that you can use when you ask questions. Then in the meeting you discuss whether you have understood correctly. The goal is to lead the conversation toward what you do and how you can help the customer.

Choose Your Sales Approach

Each buying stage often requires a different sales approach. Based on where the customer is in their buying journey when the sales process starts, the deal maker will adjust their approach accordingly. Using insights and challenging current norms is often required in every one of these approaches.

Sometimes a stakeholder may be very dissatisfied, but their boss is satisfied. In these situations it won't help you if you only approach them by diagnosing their needs, because you'll have to create pressure for those with more political power to see why they should change even if one or several stakeholders already want to buy.

You can structure your conversation in a few different ways, depending on the sales situation you are in. A presentation is not needed, but it can help in many situations especially if there are multiple attendees in the first meeting(s). The examples in the following pages show ideas of presentation material used in different sales situations. Companies often refer to this as their first call deck—adjusted based on the buyer's situation.

The three different sales approaches

"If the customer doesn't see me as a subject-matter expert, they're less likely to spend time with me or share their real concerns."

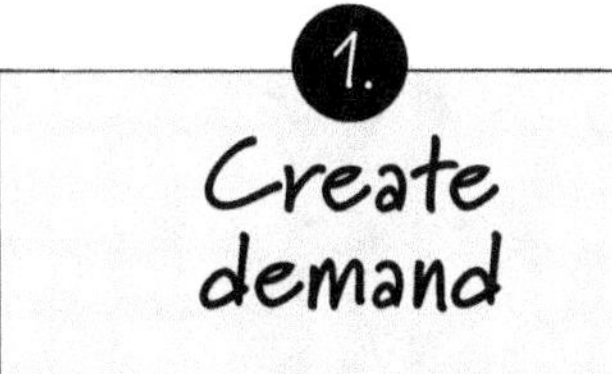

Use industry insights

In this situation, the customer does not see a need to change yet and is not interesting in investing in a solution. Use data to bring forth relevant insights and ideas about how the changes in the business environment are creating threats or possibilities for them.

Use your insights to facilitate a conversation that will help them understand why they should take action. When they begin to trust you and see a need to investigate the topics further, then you are in a great position to do discovery with them.

"As long as you're seen as credible, you can be very aggressive and challenge the customer."

"Sometimes customers don't even necessarily know which challenges they should overcome or sometimes they are not even aware that they have problems. Salespeople have to be change agents for the customers businesses."

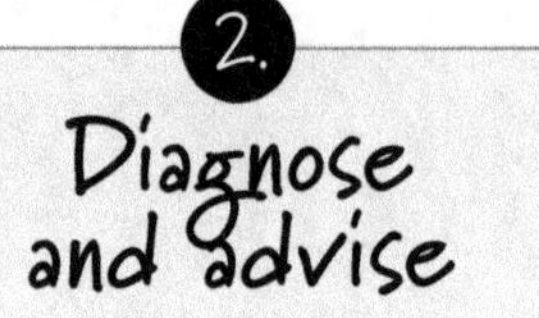

Bring insights to a specific business area or process

In some situations a customer wants to discuss specific problems, and hear how they could be solved from an external expert. They may not at this point want to do deeper discovery yet, but you will need to broaden the discussion to fully uncover how the problems connect to other business areas and what the full impact of the problems are.

It helps to use a presentation with valuable insights about the problems they are experiencing in order to get the conversation going. When you succeed you have earned the right to do a broader discovery that includes more than just diagnosing their immediate needs.

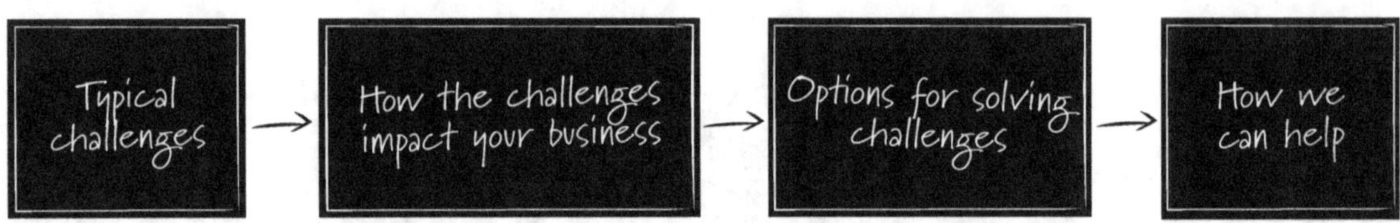

"Asking questions about pain used to be enough, but not anymore. Now you must predict the future and help the customer see what's around the corner if you want to create real value."

*"If you can find a burning fire that you can align to,
then suddenly what you are selling is a top priority."*

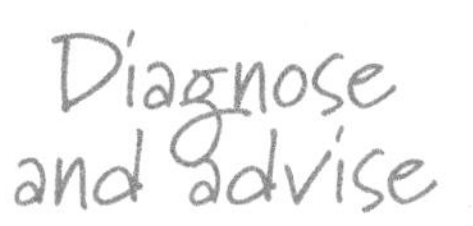

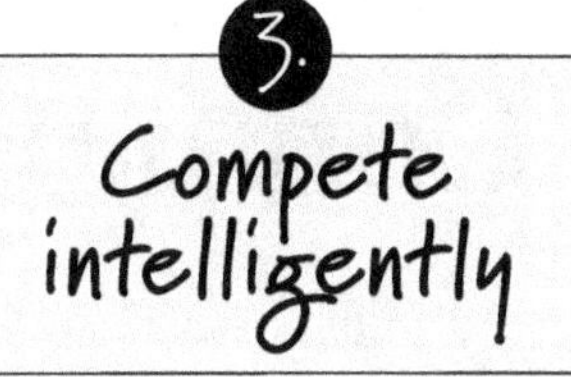

Gain Trust and Understand What The Customer Wants to Achieve

If the customer is already pretty far along in the buying process, you will most likely be competing for their time and interest with other vendors. If you can position your expertise and added value right away, you have a good chance to interest them to doing discovery before you create a proposal.

If they have already sent out an RFP, your goal is to gain enough trust to do some kind of discovery and re-evaluate their needs through analysis (more about this in the end of the "Position" part of this book).

Competing intelligently requires comprehensive analysis of your chances of winning, and then using your analysis to decide how to differentiate yourself and create more value than others.

Get Creative in a Competitive Situation!

"Randy", a strategic account manager, had decided she wanted to secure a new account. It was a major account and the last time the prospect had a competitive bidding process, it was Randy's competitor that had managed to win the deal.

The contract was coming up for bidding again, but something had changed since last time. The change was a brand new CIO and Randy knew him. She didn't know him very well, but they had previously met and Randy assumed that the CIO's attitude would be neutral and he would likely be open to discuss the upcoming RFP. Randy was right and they were able to set up a meeting at short notice.

"Can I have permission to use this slide internally?"

Randy wanted to approach this first meeting differently than the other vendors. Randy decided to create a strategy map of the prospects business for the first meeting that she would then use at some point during the meeting. The strategy map had the most important elements about the prospect's business strategy and objectives. She was able to glean this from their website and investor material found on their website.

In the strategy map, which was a one slide picture, she also included how they are seen in the media and what their business critical areas are and what the trends are in these areas. She placed speech bubbles into each part of the business strategy map with her own comments and questions.

In the beginning of the meeting with the CIO, Randy, showed a few slides about who they work with and what they've achieved, after which they discussed the prospects business pain points and challenges that had to be addressed.

Toward the end of the meeting they began to talk about why they would be the right vendor for them. That's when Randy pulled out the strategy map she had prepared in advance. First they looked at the prospects strategy and then the areas they could help them address with their portfolio. She connected the earlier discussions about the pain points and challenges to the strategy slide. Everything seemed to connect together nicely.

The CIO's comment was, "*Wow. Well, there it all is in one picture. Is it ok if I use this slide internally?*"

They ended up winning this time around and, according to the CIO, one reason was because Randy and her team wanted to understand their needs better than the other teleoperators.

Lessons Learned
Pre-meeting research and preparation was crucial for gaining trust. Since Randy was able to engage the prospect before the official bidding process, she was in a good position to influence.

Notes

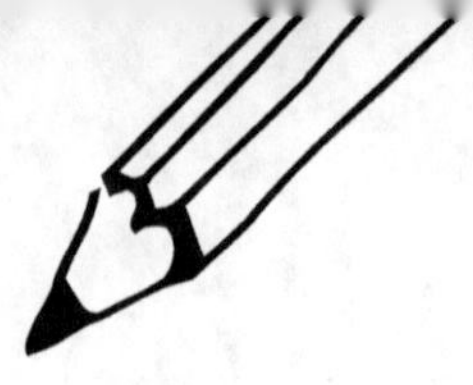

Chapter 6

Deciding How to Move Forward

Decide the Best Way Forward

The customer may only make a certain type of purchase once or perhaps just a few times during their career so they rarely have the required experience to first select the right solution, and then, implement it successfully. If you can start the sales process in the window of influence, you have a good chance to help the customer decide what the necessary steps are to ensure their purchasing process goes right.

It's the deal maker's responsibility to take charge and show the way forward. During the first meetings, it's crucial to gain commitment and create a joint way of moving forward together. The best way to do this is to establish when the desired results need to be achieved, and then work your way back to the present day. This can be referred to as back tracking.

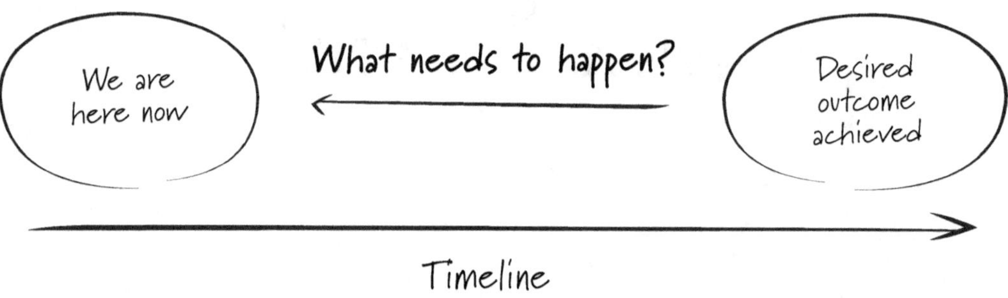

Back Tracking

A good way to gain commitment is to form a mutual timeline together by back tracking. Often once the customer realizes what a realistic timeline looks like, they realize that action must be taken much sooner than they initially thought and that there are many more things they need to do than originally imagined.

A deal maker could for example uncover that the customer wants to increase production by 5% by the end of next year. In this case the sales person could say:

"Okay, so you need to achieve a 5% increase in production within 18 months? Let's work our way back and see what needs to happen in order for us to get there."

If a deal maker shows a schedule like the one displayed on the next page, it's much easier to discuss and form a mutual timeline together with the customer by filling out the blank spots.

If during the first meeting(s), the customer is already past the first buying stage, and serious about investing, then it makes sense to use the timeline on the right to talk about what needs to happen. If you are creating demand, and therefore early in the customer's buying process, it makes sense to save this discussion about a detailed timeline for a little bit later.

At this point, either decide the next steps in detail or just the main next steps. The important thing is to set the timeline early with the prospect, to avoid costly mistakes and misunderstandings. Talking about the timeline with the prospect is used by many deal makers as a way to qualify how serious they are.

Once you start planning the details about the specific tasks and dates, these milestones form a mutual action plan (MAP). The keyword is mutual, and that means that the timeline must truly be created together with the prospect, instead of just the deal maker proposing and pushing the dates on the customer.

Sample content from a deal maker's material

Task	Date	Attendees
Interviews with key stakeholders		
Discovery workshop & technical scoping		
Business case & proposal		
Demo / lab testing/ proof of concept		
Proposal presented to management team		
Final proposal and vendor selection		
Draft of contract completed		
Legal approval		
Final agreement signed		
Project team kick-off		
Implementation of phase 1 complete		
Productivity increase achieved	Q4/2021	

Gaining a Commitment To Do Discovery

Successful deal makers are able to get their customers to want to spend more time with them, instead of their competitors. Most important stakeholders are very busy so this is not an easy task.

Since it's hard to get time from customers, a discovery process must be sold first by positioning the value of the discovery for the customer. The goal is to get the customer to commit to either doing a lighter form of discovery or heavier. A light discovery can consist of a few interviews or an extra meeting with someone that can provide more information. The benefit for the customer is that you are able to form a diagnosis of their situation and give an external point of view that will help them understand their situation and possibilities better.

A heavier discovery covers a larger amount of interviews and workshops with multiple stakeholders, often from different departments and levels within the organization, customer data analysis and typically has a formal process and a clear outcome for the customer.

"It used to be easy to get customers to do discovery workshops. Now, if we truly have something compelling to do discovery about, we can book a few quick interviews before presenting the findings. If what we find in the first interviews is interesting to the customer, then they will commit to doing a heavier discovery, like a whole day's workshop with our experts."

Gain Full Commitment Before Moving to Discovery

"Thomas," a senior account executive, was in touch with the CIO of a company that had been interested in their technology many years ago. Now, the company was in a better financial situation and the CIO said that within 12-18 months they were looking to acquire new technology. The CIO told Thomas that based on his own preliminary evaluation and knowledge of the vendors it was Thomas's company's technology or his primary competitor's technology that fit their requirements.

The CIO said that within that year he would be asking for a proposal from Thomas, and that they would internally keep working on scoping out their different requirements.

> "Either the customer fully commits to the discovery or we will lose."

Thomas's technology was definitely more advanced, and also more expensive than the competitors. He knew that it would be a very good fit with the customer's business, but he also sensed that they didn't fully yet appreciate and understand what their technology platform could do for them. Thomas knew he needed to gain access to the most important stakeholders and build a business case and a demo that showed each key stakeholder how the platform could help their individual departments. The CIO had told Thomas that his team would be in charge of running the project and that the stakeholders would not be actively be involved in the process with the two vendor candidates.

Thomas knew this was a problem, because he needed to understand the stake-holders' challenges better. He would not have a good chance at winning against his competitor if he couldn't change the customer's approach.

Thomas thought that he had to get the customer to fully commit to the discovery process or he'd lose the deal. In a conversation with the CIO, he conveyed:

"If we're going to answer the RFP, I want to give you the best possible understanding of what we can offer. This means we need to really understand your business requirements and then give you a great demo. This should help you with the requirements you outline in the RFP. Our experts will need to be able to interview your business stakeholders, and these same people will need to be present in the workshops and demos to give their comments. Usually these stakeholders learn from our interview findings, because we can give them ideas of best practices based on what our other customers are doing."

After weeks of hesitation, the CIO agreed that this approach would be acceptable and committed to arranging the different workshops. He promised to make sure different key stakeholders would also attend the workshops. A few months later, the RFP was issued and four months after that, they finally won the deal.

Lessons Learned

It was a tough sales project for Thomas and his pre-sales engineer, but they ended up winning because they got the customer to properly commit to doing a discovery. If they hadn't done discovery, they would have missed the perspectives of several really important stakeholders. The value proposition wouldn't have been as strong, and their competitor who was the preferred vendor before the RFP was sent would have won. The discovery also allowed the business stakeholders to learn that this should not be an IT-driven project, and that the business leaders would have to be highly involved in the implementation if they wanted to succeed.

Notes

Qualify Before Investing More Time

Is This Opportunity Really Worth Pursuing?

Just because a first meeting (or several first meetings) go well and the fit seems good, it doesn't mean the customer will necessarily buy. The best deal makers critically analyze if the opportunity is worth going after. You always have to be able to disengage and qualify out if the customer is not willing to invest their time and resources to further pursue the opportunity. As one of those interviewed said:

> "It takes two to tango. You should never be afraid, or so desperate to win a deal, that you cannot qualify out or disengage if your normal criteria is not fulfilled."

In situations where you are uncertain, you can tell the customer how you see the situation and see how they react. Based on their reaction, you can keep working or politely disengage from the opportunity. For example, you could say something like this if you think the opportunity is weak:

> "This is what we're seeing... maybe we are not the right partner for you. Do you agree?"

Qualifying Opportunities

Qualification should be based on evidence you have, so that you can as objectively as possible evaluate whether you should pursue the opportunity or not.

> "You never have an opportunity without pain and a champion."

Qualifying Budget & Timeline

At this point deal makers mostly focus on solution fit & relationships strength as the main guiding factors in qualification.

Budget and timeline are good to bring into the qualification as well, but should not be the main guiding points. Budget is made available if there is something important enough to invest in and the right people want to invest. If you have strong relationships you are able to create the budget. Budget and timeline become easy to discuss, when there is a big enough need and relationship strength is strong.

Solution Fit

Is there enough serious pain now or projected pain in the future that would justify an investment?

How well does our portfolio fit what they need & have we helped customers in this situation before?

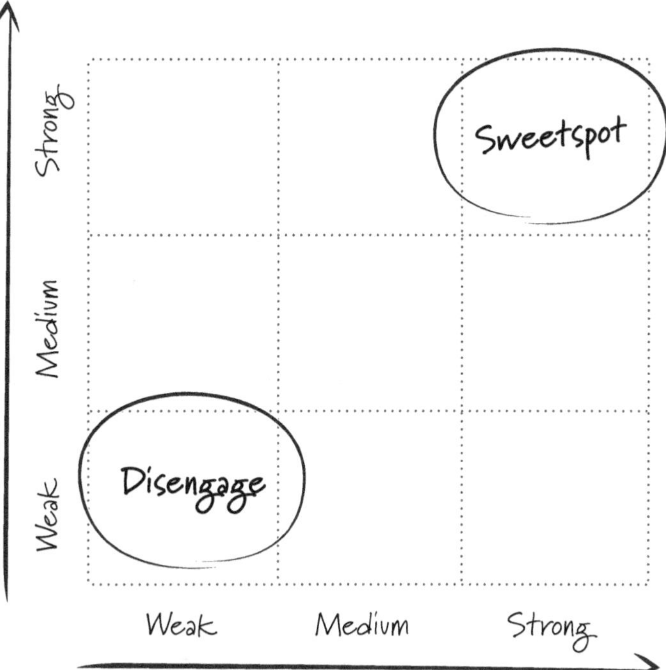

"If a deal I'm working on is not a great fit for what we do, and we don't yet have access to power, I always approach with extreme caution"

Relationship Strength

Are we talking to the stakeholders who are responsible for the areas where the problems are being experienced?

Can we gain access to the right people and get them involved?

The Power of Relationships

A sales executive named "Felicia" created a list of potential customers for a new production output technology her company recently acquired.

Felicia noticed that a prospect's CIO was connected to their company's CEO on Linkedin. Felicia did a bit more background research and ended up finding out that the CEO actually knew the CIO very well. Since they were planning a launch event for this new technology, Felicia wanted to invite the CIO. Felicia, who had a good relationship with the CEO, requested that the CEO personally send an invite to the CIO to make sure he attended.

The CIO came to the event and brought the VP of Production with him. At the event, when Felicia had a chance to talk to the CIO and VP, they actually said that they had been looking at this type of technology a while back, but they didn't think the timing was right at that point. Based on what they saw at the event, they thought now could be a good idea to re-evaluate their situation.

Felicia proposed that they do a demo and presentation so that a broader group of people could quickly gain an understanding of the benefits of the new technology. She knew the demo was not important in order to get the sale, but it would get the discussions going. This approach was accepted and a few weeks later they had a meeting with a big group of stakeholders. After this they ended up getting the right stakeholders more involved and they did several discovery workshops and about ten months later they had reached an agreement and began implementing the technology.

Creating an opportunity plan

An opportunity plan (also referred to as a "win plan") is created when you decide to pursue an opportunity. Deal Makers typically create an opportunity plan after the first few meetings when the opportunity is qualified. In the beginning there are many gaps in the plan, but as you move further in the process, the missing parts are filled with information as you learn more about the customer.

The goal of the plan is to have a document that clearly explains how the Deal Maker and his/her team will win. The plan helps identify any gaps in the planned actions points and helps pinpoint potential red flags as early as possible in the sales process. Often the opportunity plan is also an important instrument in communicating internally with all members of the team that are working on the opportunity.

The plan should include the details of what needs to happen on the customer's side before they are able to sign a contract. Later the action items in the opportunity can be confirmed as you create a mutual action plan with your champion.

It's the details of the plan and their validity that sets the best opportunities plans apart from the rest. Knowing more about the customer, allows you to navigate more efficient from start to close.

"To win deals you need to have deal vision. This means having a clear vision of the value you will create and how you differentiate yourself from your competitors."

> Living document that explains how you will win the deal

"Victorious warriors win first and then go to war, while defeated warriors go to war first and then seek to win."

—Sun Tzu

Opportunity Plan Content

- The customer's strategy & financial goals

- Objectives & business issues

- Solution fit and solution scope

- Compelling reasons to purchase now

- Win theme

- Key stakeholders involved and their roles in the buying process

- Relationships with the key stakeholders

- Team & responsibilities

- Strengths & weaknesses against their other options

- Customer's buying process (official and unofficial)

- Identified risks

- Action plan with tasks and dates

Checklist

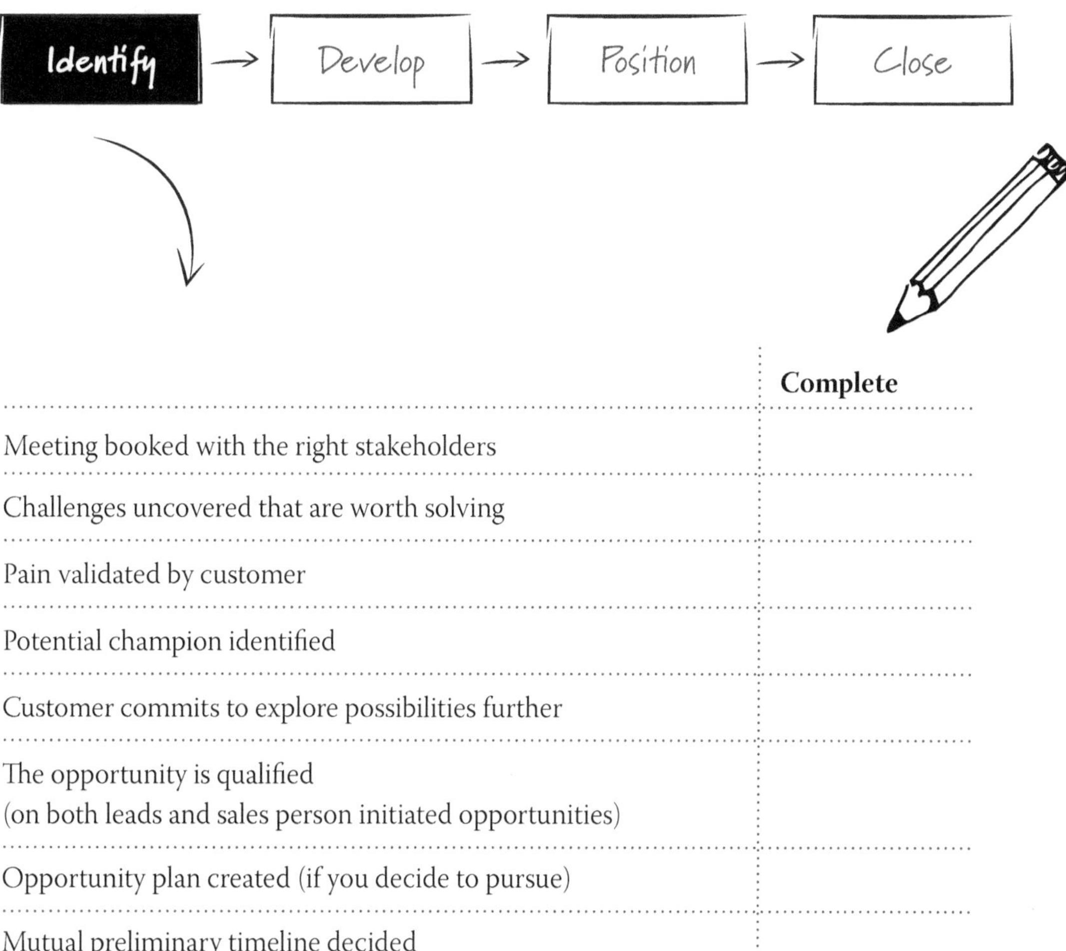

Complete

Meeting booked with the right stakeholders

Challenges uncovered that are worth solving

Pain validated by customer

Potential champion identified

Customer commits to explore possibilities further

The opportunity is qualified
(on both leads and sales person initiated opportunities)

Opportunity plan created (if you decide to pursue)

Mutual preliminary timeline decided

Notes

PART II
Develop

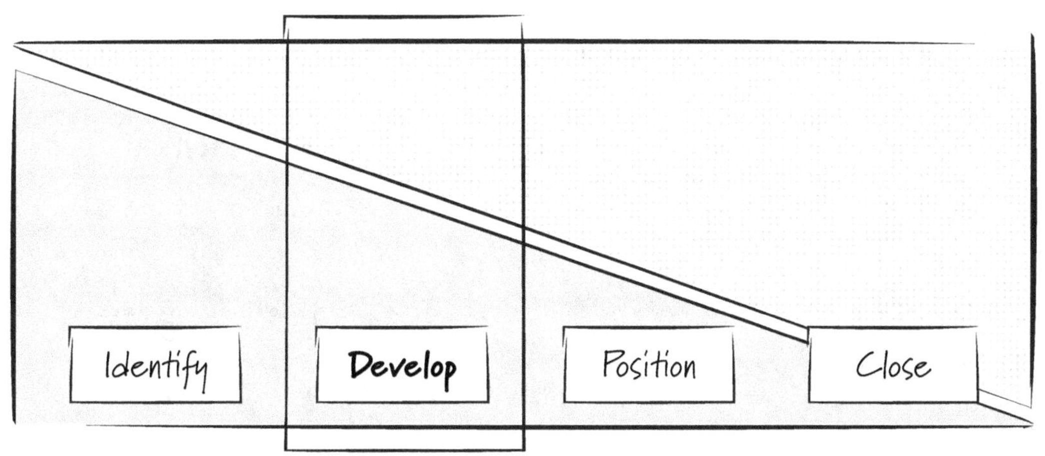

"Take the customer on a journey."

The Main Goals of this Stage

Create value for the customer

Gain access and create relationships with key stakeholders involved in decision making

Achieve a strong understanding of the customer's business landscape & market

Understand the customer's strategy, financial goals and objectives

Identify problems & their financial impact

Evaluate Your Deal Making Habits

How do you maximize the value you create throughout the sales process before creating a proposal?

How do you uncover information about the customer's most important objectives and measurable problems?

How do you find and gain the trust of a true champion?

How do you make sure you engage all important stakeholders in the right way?

Analyze Your Current Situation Before Doing Discovery

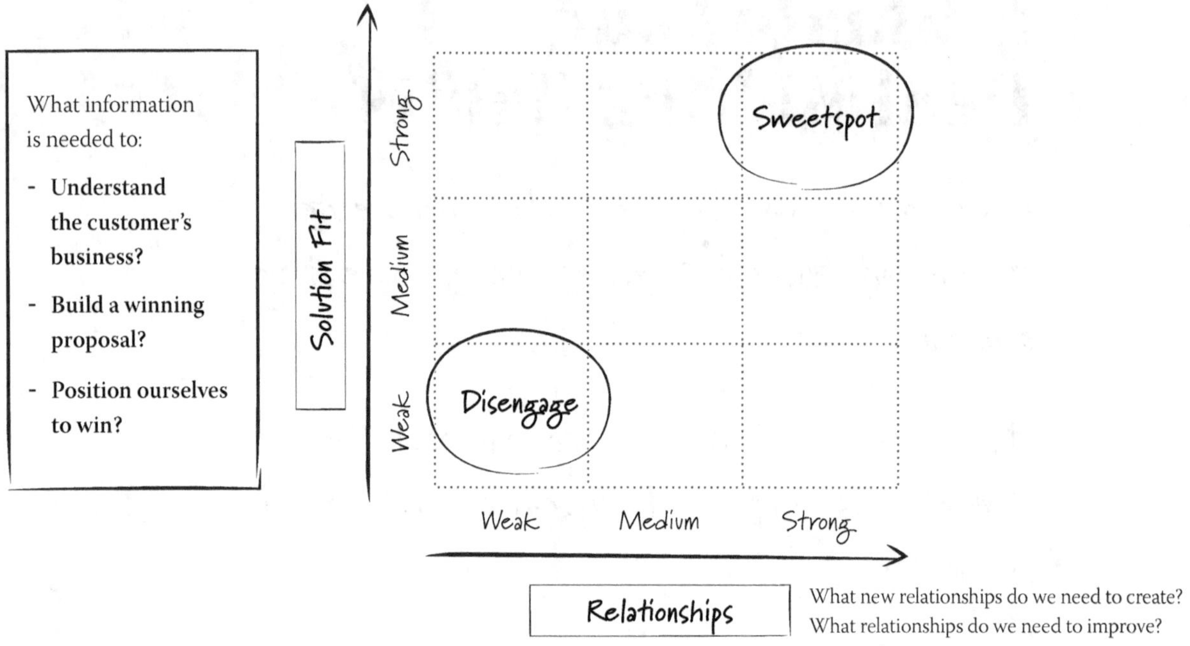

Without the right relationships you will not be able to get enough information to position your solution, even if it is a great fit. That's why so many deal makers emphasize the importance of understanding and developing relationships with different stakeholders.

In the next chapter, we'll cover relationships followed by the business value discovery. Discovery with the wrong stakeholders can be an enormous waste of time, so that's why we will cover the relationship aspect first.

Out of the over 100 deals that were analyzed for the research, most of them hinged on relationships as opposed to how good the fit was.

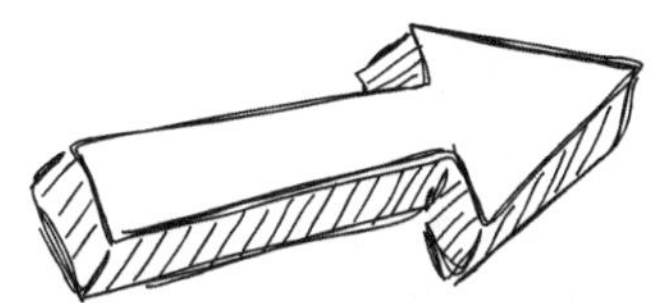

Chapter 7

Facilitating the Complex Sale

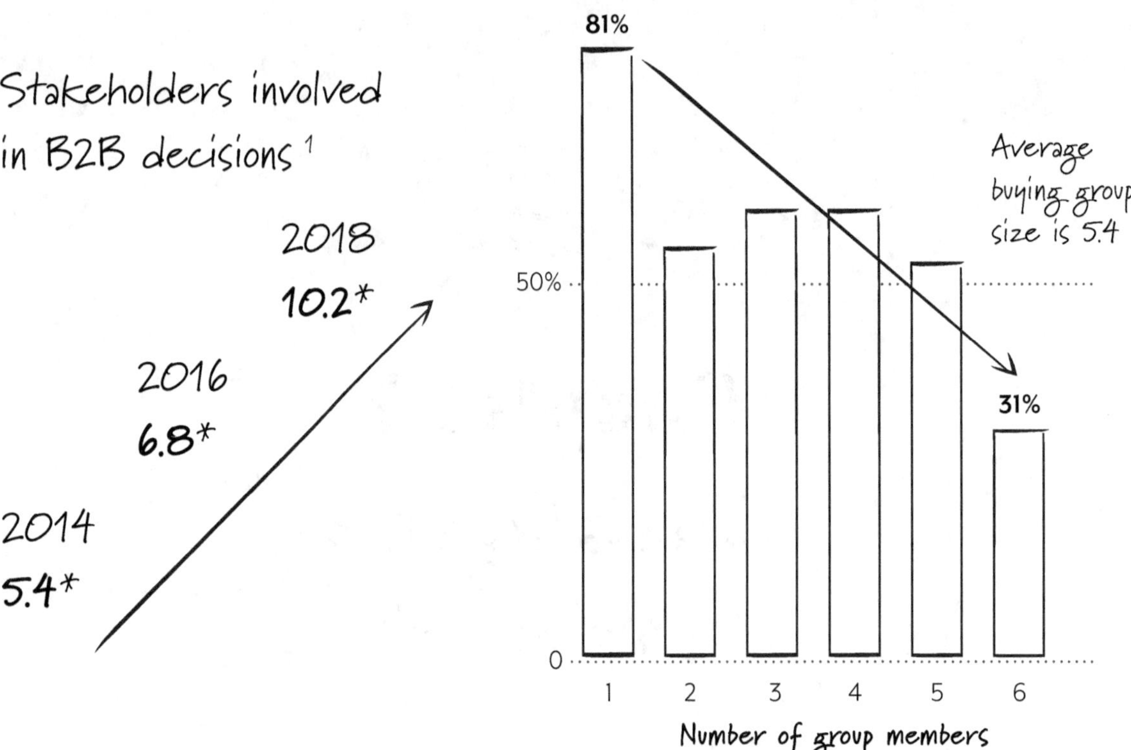

Original research by CEB/Motista (2013 B2B Brand survey)

In the past 10 years there has been a considerable increase in the amount of stakeholders involved in B2B decisions. As the buying group size increases, it brings down the likelihood of a purchase happening, because finding consensus in a larger group is more difficult. The larger and more complex the deal, the more stakeholders will be involved.

More Stakeholders Increase Complexity

Each stakeholder has their unique point of view and personal motivators. Deal makers have to include stakeholders from several departments. Buying a solution that impacts several different departments means that those departments must have a shared view of the problem as well as a shared agreement on what the best way to solve the problem(s) are.

In the beginning of the buying process, the people that are the most concerned are involved. Then their managers and end-users get involved. Then procurement, legal, IT and other support functions. All the way to the end of the process, the management team (and potentially even the board) has a say in the purchase. As you move forward, there are always people joining who have a say in things.

Of course it doesn't have to be in this sequence, because the best deal makers are often able to involve stakeholders in powerful positions early in the sales process. If they are not able to involve the right stakeholders early enough, there is a risk that the sales process is moving forward prematurely.

"75% of B2B customers agree or strongly agree that their purchase involved people from a wide variety of roles, teams and locations." [2]

Understanding Hidden Politics

When there aren't major differences between the vendors solutions, the customer will most often prefer working with those they like and trust more. The most experienced sales leaders I've talked to highlight how their most successful deal makers have an incredible ability to create relationships at high-levels. A relationship doesn't have to mean you become friends, but you create relationships of trust & respect. Trust with a wide range of stakeholders becomes a key factor in winning larger deals. **Building relationships is at the core of complex deals!**

Understanding hidden internal politics

A successful deal maker must understand customer politics because it's a major factor in how complex decisions are made. Having the right relationships helps achieve this deeper understanding of the customer.

It's very hard to uncover and understand internal politics. That's why it's so crucial to have a champion(s) within the customers organization. They may not directly explain how things are, but reading between the lines and listening for quiet signals in each conversation can help put the puzzle together and help in understanding the hidden political dynamics of the organization. There are many factors going on behind the scenes that average and poor sales people don't understand. For example things like: Who chose the previous solution, who is up for a promotion, and who is at risk of being fired.

It's not in the buyer's interest to "show all their cards." Therefore, many stakeholders often withhold essential information from external vendors. A skilled deal maker carefully listens and analyzes different situations, while a poor salesperson takes what the certain stakeholders tell them as the truth.

Difficulties of Hidden Dynamics

"Andy," a senior account executive at a leading software company was contacted by a technology implementation partner. One of their big customers was interested in buying the type of software Andy sold. This company was a globally spread out manufacturer that needed to buy new software to manage their customers better in order to achieve their growth targets.

Both Andy and his sales engineer worked on the opportunity together with the partner. Everything went smoothly because the partner had a very strong relationship with key stakeholders in the management team responsible for selecting the right vendor. One of the key stakeholders was the head of the buying committee; he was also the leader of the business unit that was going to use the software. The other key stakeholder was the CIO.

> The two main stakeholders in the buying committee just did not have enough political power.

According to the buying committee, Andy's solution had the best demo and solution presentation, and they were chosen as the preferred vendor by the buying committee. They had a powerful business sponsor and IT-sponsor (or so they thought).

The two main stakeholders in the buying committee presented their #1 preference to the management team, which is when things went south. They called Andy the next day and told him they were sorry, but their decision was "overruled in the management team."

The leader of another business division that was their growth star (clearly growing faster and the future of the company), opposed the purchase. This leader had never attended any workshops or presentations until the decision. Andy didn't think the leader was going to be a major influencer in the purchase decision because the solution wasn't going to be used by his division.

The hidden leader had implemented a certain technology platform a few years earlier for his division. This technology had different modules that could be used for various different business functions. The leader wanted the other departments to use the optional modules that his chosen technology platform offered, even though they didn't fully fit the requirements. He wanted this because he didn't want his chosen technology to be at risk of getting less resources and he wanted to keep working without distractions and keep executing their own chosen IT strategy.

The CEO who was the ultimate decision-maker understood that if this new technology was introduced to the other division, it would mean less synergies between the divisions. That might mean the more important division would potentially get less IT resources. The CEO didn't want to risk irritating or losing the trust of the leader of the most important division that was profitable and growing.

Andy's technology was better but that wasn't enough in the CEO's mind to offset the risk of irritating the new leader and having him potentially leave the company. The CEO was counting on that leader to develop and lead the business for many years to come.

Lessons Learned

The two main stakeholders in the buying committee just did not have enough political power and capability to influence the management team. They were too weak in the management team to get approval for what they thought was the right decision. A critical (hidden) stakeholder was left outside the sales process. A buying committee does not necessarily have the final buying power.

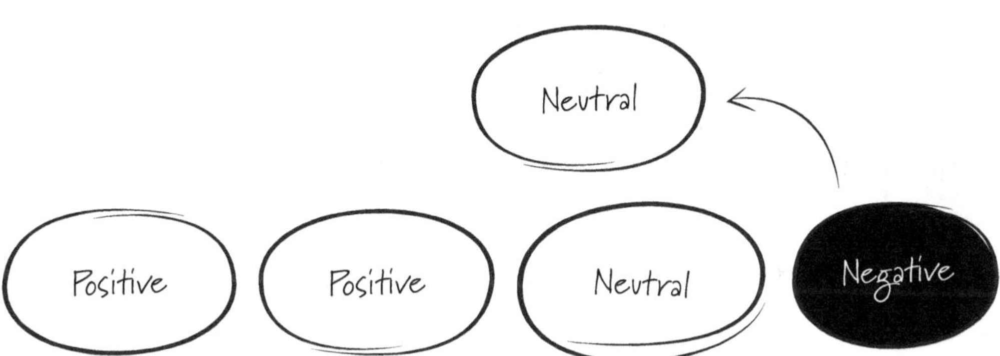

Decision making team

Facilitating the Buying Process of Multiple Stakeholders

What matters in big purchases is what the customer and their organization does, as well as how they move forward in the buying stages. Pushing a deal forward and doing the things outlined in a typical sales process doesn't actually mean that a customer's buying process is proceeding.

The deal maker's goal is to help the customer make a good and safe decision. This means maximizing the value of the solution, while minimizing risks of a bad decision, and also, helping them avoid costly mistakes in the implementation of the solution.

The more complex the purchase is, the less likely it is that the customer has lots of experience in making such a purchase. The risk of failure is high and buying in a situation like this can be very stressful and time consuming. In purchases that business stakeholders do not often make, they do not have a buying process so how they come up with the requirements can be greatly impacted by a trusted advisor (the deal maker). The deal maker is in a great position to be the preferred choice when they can help with the buying process.

"A stakeholder that wants to purchase a solution may only make this decision once in their life. We help customers implement these solutions every day and know the buying and implementation process by heart, so we're in a great position to help the customer with the buying process."

Notes

What you see here is a slide used by a deal maker early in the sales process to help the customer with their overall buying process. This was presented to the customer one month before the event in June, which is the first milestone on the timeline. The customer had not yet created a plan for evaluating the different vendor options. Based on this draft of a timeline, the deal maker and customer created a mutual action plan.

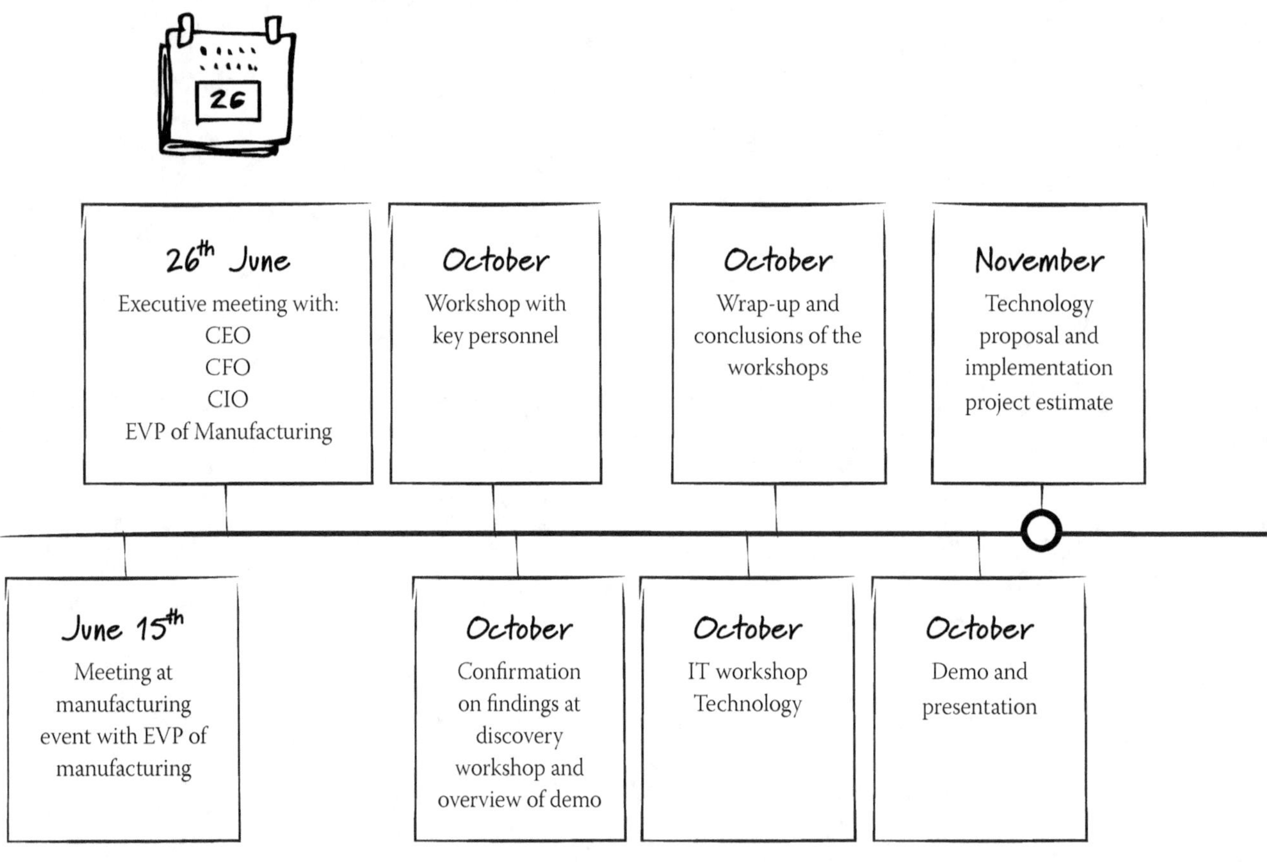

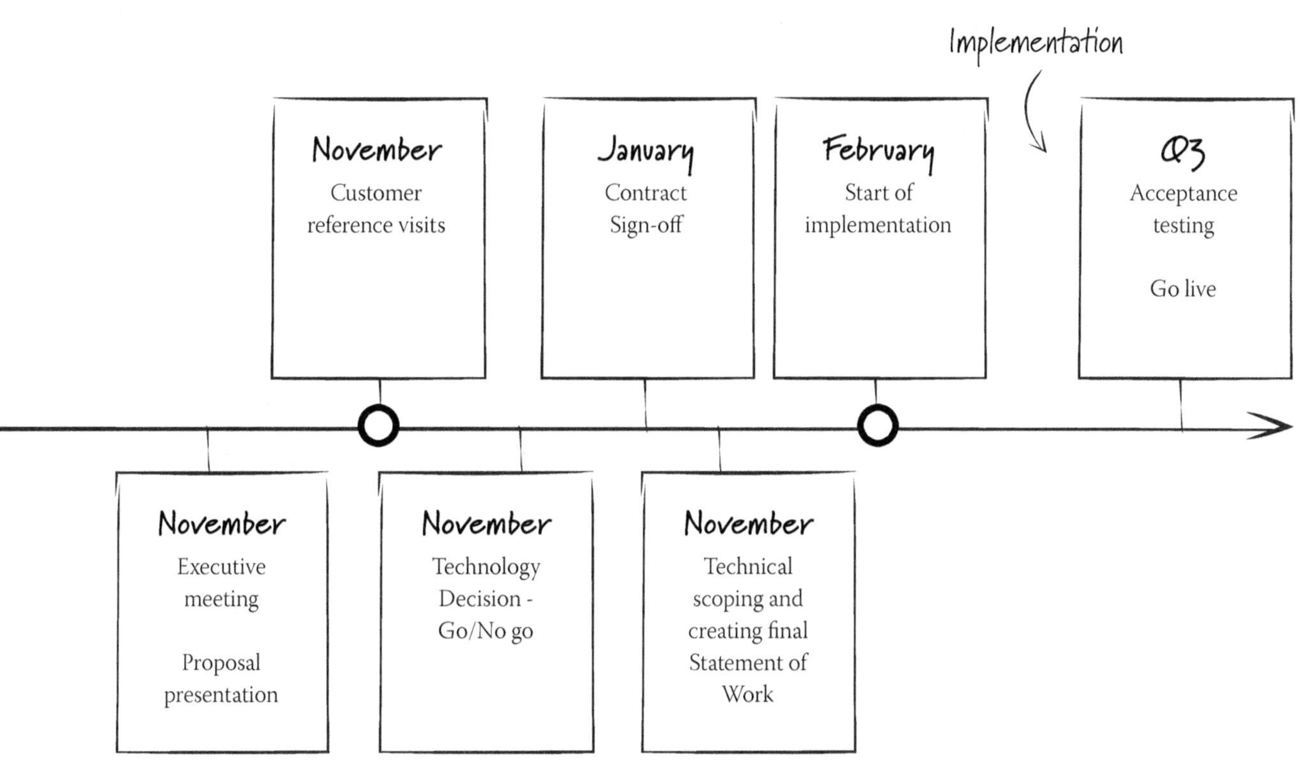
Implementation

November
Customer
reference visits

January
Contract
Sign-off

February
Start of
implementation

Q3
Acceptance
testing

Go live

November
Executive
meeting

Proposal
presentation

November
Technology
Decision -
Go/No go

November
Technical
scoping and
creating final
Statement of
Work

Notes

Chapter 8

Developing Relationships

Building the Right Relationships During Discovery

Getting to power as early and as fast as possible, is something most experienced deal makers strive for. If they don't yet have access to power, they figure out how to get access. You do not want to be stuck on the operative level where decision are not made. This is what a few interviewed deal makers said about reaching decision-makers:

"Aim for the stars and only spend your time with people who actually make things happen in their organizations."

"You need to spend time with the people who are putting their money on the table."

"The CFO or CIO may be a lame duck. They may be a person with a title, but no power. You need to understand the personalities that are in play and their political power."

Engaging the Right Stakeholders in Discovery

What different stakeholder's focus on

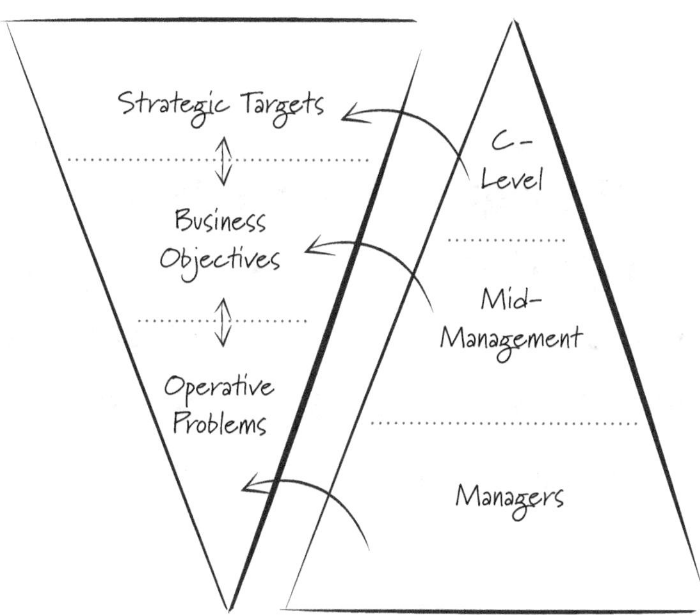

When doing discovery, if you ask strategic questions from people that don't have insights about the company's strategy, then you are at risk of not being able to position yourself with initiatives that upper management considers important.

If you want valid information you have to engage the right stakeholders that have the right information. If it's not possible to get information directly from the most powerful stakeholders, target stakeholders who work as closely as possible with the real decision makers

"It's not just access at the right level that is important. What's even more important is access to the right person, who understands all the different variables and factors that go into making a large decision of this nature."

The Priority List

The CxO level has certain priorities, but everyone doesn't necessarily know within the organization exactly how things are prioritized. Imagine the customer had one priority list, and you must be able to get what you are selling on to the top of that list if you want to win a big deal. There is a cut-off line and below the cut-off line are good ideas worth pursuing, but not right now. These ideas below the line may be revisited next year or the year after that, or completely taken off the list later.

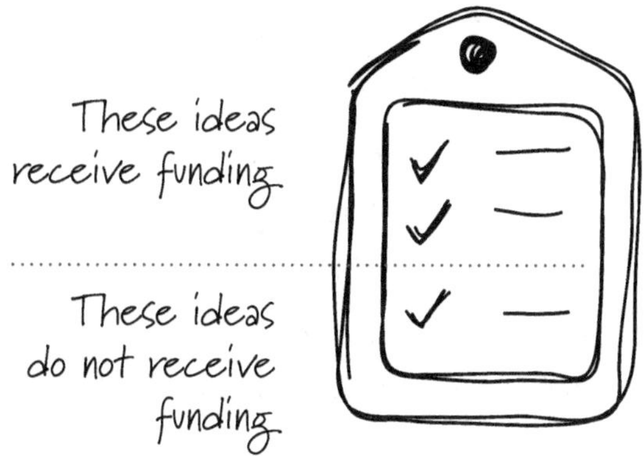

Often you may need to bump other priorities down below the cut-off line in order to get what you are selling funded.

If management doesn't know about the project you are pursuing and is not involved, there is a huge risk that what you are selling is not aligned with their top priorities.

Lack of Power

"Ken," a software account executive, was selling to a large corporation and his key point of contact was the CIO. He was very sure that he would win because he had a good relationship with the CIO and the CIO had already verbally agreed he would give Ken the business. The CIO was the person who would give the final authorization and sign the agreement.

Ken had this deal in his forecast for many months, just waiting for the final contract to be signed. After a few months, the VP of sales started wondering why the deal had been sitting in the same forecast category for so long. Ken assured the VP of sales it was going to close because the CIO told them they were the preferred vendor and he was going to give them the contract. The CIO relayed to Ken that there were some internal delays temporarily stalling the project.

> "We have decided we're not going to do this project, but we just haven't told the CIO yet."

The VP of sales wanted to get another point of view so he ended up calling the customer's CEO (a contact the VP already knew). What the VP heard from the CEO presented a serious challenge: "We have decided we're not going to do this project, but we just haven't told the CIO yet."

Lessons Learned

If you are not talking to true power, you will often not have the latest and most accurate information.

Notes

Stakeholder Onion

Stakeholder layers involved in making a purchasing decision

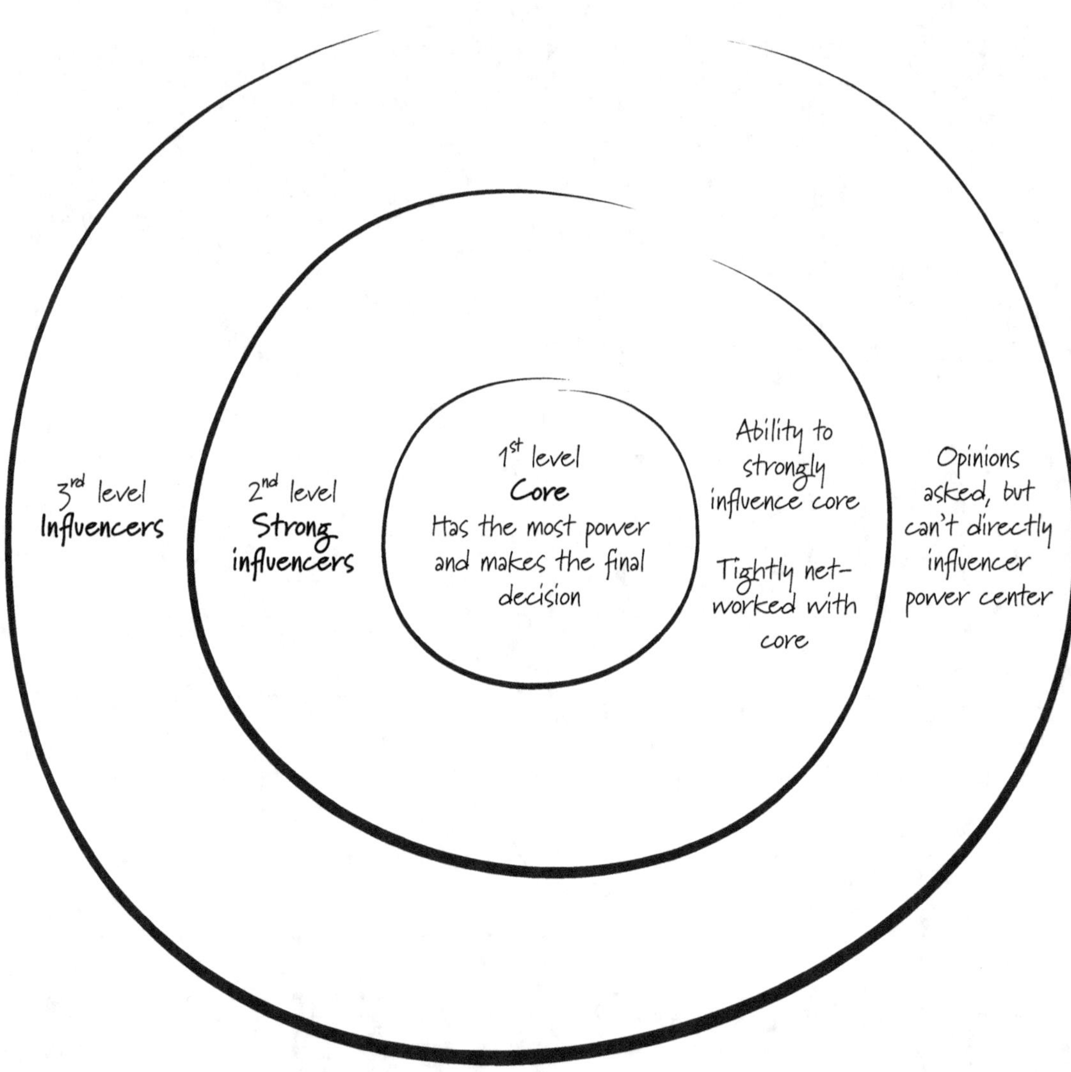

Deal makers need to understand all the stakeholders, but they focus on stakeholders with political power and incentive to make things happen. In complex deals there is seldomly such a thing as a single decision-maker. The closer to the middle you get, the better your chances are to influence decision-making.

Beware, the 2nd and 3rd levels can have both weak and strong political power. It's not so easy to recognize who has and who doesn't have strong political power.

"The differences between winning and losing hinges on understanding the decision-making mindset of the customer. Winning a deal comes down to individual motivations and incentives. Having a product that fits their requirements is only for table stakes."

"In hindsight, I really didn't know what was going on behind the scenes when I lost deals in the past."

Identifying and Engaging Different Stakeholders

Amount of Stakeholders Typically Involved

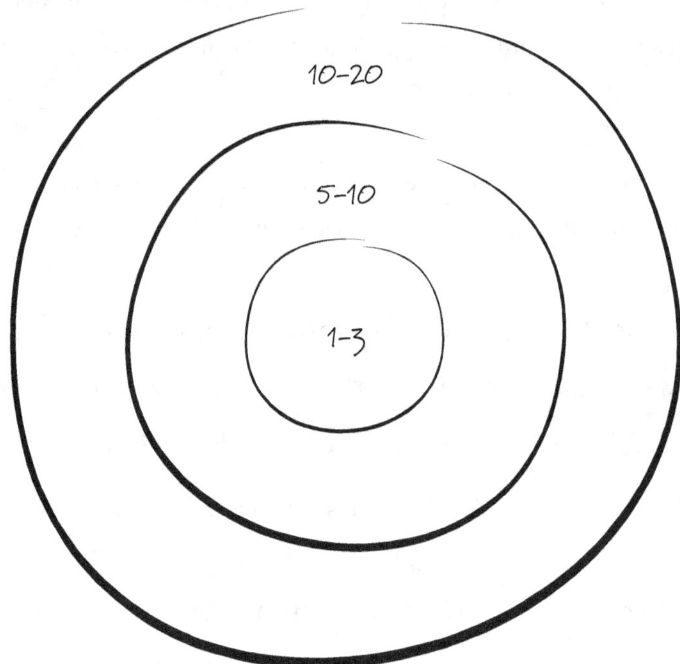

When the interviewed deal makers were asked how many stakeholders are typically involved in their deals, the average was around 10-25.

Of course this depended on the deal size & size of organization they were selling to. When selling to small and medium businesses, there could be between 1-5 stakeholders involved, while enterprise deals may involve 10-50 stakeholders.

Identifying Stakeholders with a Motive

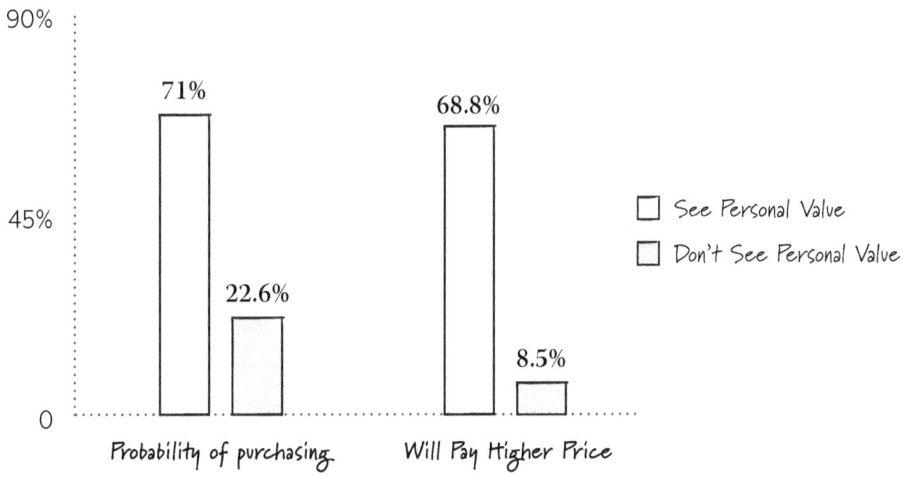

Original research by CEB/Motista (2013 B2B Brand survey)

Those that will benefit personally from your solution not only want to buy from you, but they are also willing to pay more for what you are selling. The goal is to understand the personal agenda and motivators of each stakeholder. Personal motivators could for example be: career advancement, saving time and spending more time with family, recognition within the company etc.

Often many stakeholders will not see personal value, because they do not understand the value of solving certain problems or the value of solving them in a certain way. In this case it's the deal makers responsibility to educate them and help them understand.

One interviewed deal maker pointed out: *"Facts make customers think, but only emotion makes them act"*. This deal makers point was that if you cannot get anyone emotionally involved, then you have very low chances of winning a profitable deal.

Key Stakeholders

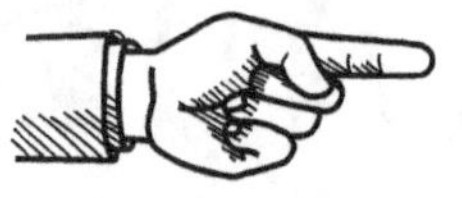

Executive Sponsor

Typically in the C-level and responsible for the part of the business that your solution will impact the most

Must be on your side if you want to win the deal

Responsible for the project outcome and results

Often the champion is one notch below the executive sponsor, and reports directly to him/her

Champion

A champion needs to be a strong influencer with some political power, otherwise they are just a coach. At some point in the sales process the Champion becomes your salesperson on the inside. Having a champion is important to be able to influence those you cannot directly reach easily, for example, the C-suite.

Once the project is successful the champion becomes the hero and accelerates his/her career forward.

Without a champion diffusing roadblocks, helping you navigate through the toughest situations later in the sales process, selling is like driving a car with a blindfold on.

Coach

Coaches are often interested in what you are selling, but are in weak political positions. A coach can guide and share some information, but will not do any selling on your part because they cannot do any heavy lifting internally to make things happen.

Beware of coaches disguised as champions.

"A champion is someone who is as passionate and excited as you are, which means they will go to the management team or board and fight to get funding for the project."

"When you are selling enterprise deals,
there are various factors and politics involved.
If you don't have a champion to guide you,
you will fail."

Gaining a Foothold Through the Champion

A service company wanted to develop their profitability by increasing the efficiency of their field service engineers. They created a long-list of different potential vendors and then eventually boiled it down to a short-list of only a few vendors they wanted to engage with to discuss more about their capabilities.

"Matt," an account executive, was assigned to this lead and started the discussions with someone who *"could never have placed an order,"* but this person was in charge of evaluating the different solutions out in the marketplace that would fit their needs. It was his boss that would eventually make the final decision once different options, along with their pros and cons, were understood.

> Once the development manager was certain the solution was a good fit he started warming up to arranging a meeting to present to his boss.

The person who was in charge of evaluating the vendor options was the development manager and he had a very good grip of the operational challenges that had to be fixed. In order to understand what they were trying to achieve and why, as well as gain a deep understanding of the problems in the processes, Matt proposed that they do a workshop before creating a demonstration of his solutions capabilities.

Once the development manager was certain that Matt's solution was a good fit he started warming up to arranging a meeting to present to his boss. He could clearly see that the solution would make his boss a hero when implemented correctly. Matt knew that this was now his chance to truly help this opportunity move forward.

In the next meeting with the boss who was the CEO, they showed a demo, but instead of placing focus on the technology, Matt shifted the discussion to the service company's vision and strategy and their under-lying obstacles that were preventing them from success. Matt knew, he would succeed, if they were able to focus on how they should develop the business, insteading of getting too technical. In this meeting, trust was build with the CEO and with a rapid pace from there on, they proceeded to winning the contract.

Lessons Learned:

- Matt was able to team up with someone who would eventually guide him to power.

- Access to power was earned, but it was the plan from the beginning to be able to talk to the C-level about their goals and business challenges.

- Without a relationship with the CEO who held the ultimate power in this opportunity, Matt's chances of winning the deal would have dropped dramatically.

Earning Your Champion

You don't just find a champion. You earn the right stakeholder's trust and slowly they will become your champion, once you prove you can add value to their organization (and to them personally).

At this point everything becomes easier, because you can cooperate with someone on the customer's side who has a network within the company that you can tap into.

"As a sales person, you can only believe so much from a 10-K report or corporate profile summary. You need someone on the inside to help you understand what is really going on behind the scenes."

Working With Your Champion

Before the official purchasing process starts (Window of Influence) is the right time to understand the informal and formal process of purchasing within the company. Understanding both the formal and informal is a must and without a champion this becomes near to impossible for the sales person.

Towards the end of the official purchasing process, the champion will give the deal maker information "under the table" that helps make last minute improvements and react to risks and make adjustments to proposals. They will even sell to other stakeholders internally on behalf of the deal maker.

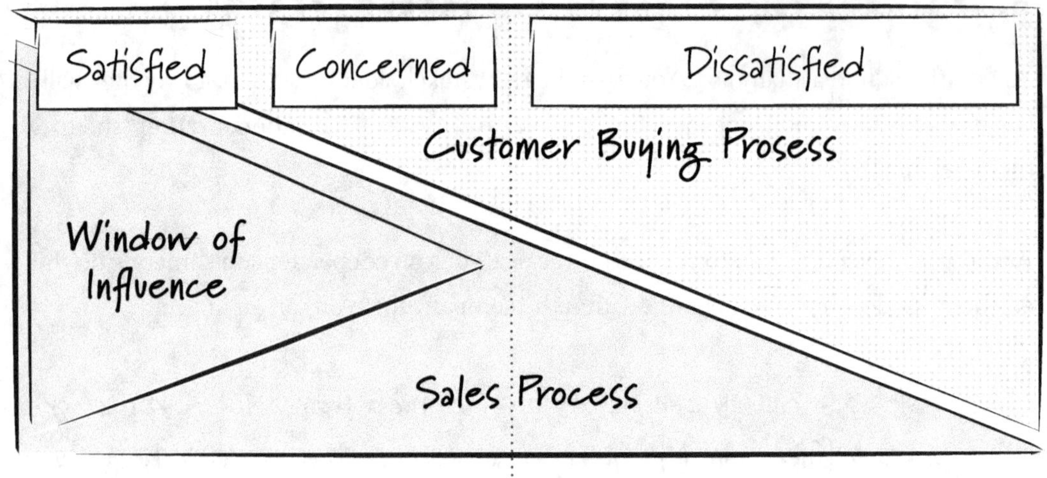

Start cooperating with a champion	Work together with your champion to win the deal

Notes

....

....

....

....

....

....

Test Your Champion

It's not always easy to recognize if you have a strong champion or just a coach. Many of the deal makers interviewed talked about testing to see if they are truly working with a champion, instead of a coach.

Here are some ideas for testing your champion:

- Ask them to do something difficult and see if they will do it

- Request them to set up a meeting with someone higher in the organization and see how they react

- Ask them to deliver or create some sort of material

- Ask them for contact information to others within the organization

Small signals to expect from a champion:

- Sharing confidential or sensitive information even if you don't ask

- Calling outside of office hours

- Text messaging from internal meetings

Deal making and working with a champion is about getting someone else to commit to a series of actions. It all starts with small commitments that lead to increasingly larger commitments until you get the final commitment, aka the contract.

Moving the Right Stakeholders Forward in the Buying Process

Buying Stages →

Stakeholder Role	Title	Satisfied (Doesn't think there is any need)	Concerned (aware of problems, but not ready to buy)	Dissatisfied (supports the investment decision)
Final Approver	CEO	X		
Executive Sponsor	CFO		X	
Project Owner	VP Sales			X
Buyer/ Procurement	Procurement Manager	X		
Technical Approver	CIO	X		

Here you see the buying stages that were introduced earlier. Although some stakeholders may want to buy, other very important stakeholders are often not ready. This was a major reason why deal makers lost deals early in their careers. The goal of the deal maker is to move the right stakeholders forward in their buying stages. Neglecting to engage a certain stakeholder in the buying process can mean they will stall the deal or not support the buying decision.

Quick Stakeholder Analysis:

1. Who are all the main stakeholders that should be involved?

2. What are the stakeholders roles in the buying process?

3. At which buying stages are the different stakeholders?

4. Have you met the different stakeholders? Yes/no

5. Are they all on your side? Yes/no

The best deal makers are adept at identifying who they need to engage with and will do what it takes to move the right stakeholders forward in the buying stages.

Bringing Important Stakeholders Along for the Buying Ride!

"Sam," a major account manager of a technology company had been engaged with a bank for many months, working on something that could potentially be highly innovative and would differentiate the bank from its competitors.

Sam was working with the CDO, also the main project leader, as well as the IT director. The CDO was already on Sam's side and the IT director seemed neutral. The IT director told Sam and her team about several details that were important for his team. They were acknowledged by Sam and her team, but not properly analyzed and later forgotten, because they weren't seen as crucial for the success of the project. When it was time to make a decision, the CDO wanted to buy, but the IT director had made up his mind that he wanted a different solution and forced them to chose the competing solution.

It later became apparent that there were certain technical show-stoppers regarding Sam's technology that would mean the IT director would have to make changes to his current IT architecture, which he was strictly against.

The safer solution covered a smaller amount of the CDO's requirements but also meant less risk and less work for the IT director's team—it was the solution that was chosen, and later, implemented.

Lessons Learned

After losing this deal, Sam realized she should have properly gone through the IT-director's requirements and validated his concerns. She wasn't able to visualize how the decision making dynamics would play out. She didn't realize that the IT director had so much power and assumed that the CDO would be able to make a decision, even without the strong support of the IT-director.

"Matt," a sales manager, was sure he was going to win a big deal. All the needed documents had been submitted. Pricing got approval several weeks earlier; they had gone through numerous rounds of presenting to the management team and owners whom supported them to go ahead and work on the final contract. The customer was reviewing the contract two days before they had planned to sign, when Matt got a phone call from the CEO saying, "We don't think this deal is going to happen." The operations' manager had said that she was not comfortable moving forward. She believed that the other option they had been looking at would be better.

Even though the CEO thought Matt's solution was the right option for them, he ultimately trusted the operations' manager and if she didn't believe it could work then they couldn't proceed. The CEO decided to ask Matt to talk to her.

Matt contacted the operations' manager the same day. He was able to get her to explain her point of view. She felt that if the system didn't work as promised, it would reflect negatively on her because her team would be managing the implementation. She didn't believe that the solution would work and therefore wouldn't deliver the desired results because she didn't yet understand how everything fit together with their processes and Matt's solution. Matt reassured her that the issues she had raised were getting a lot of attention internally and that they were very important to them. Matt said his company was going to have their best resources helping them with the implementation and they would get the needed extra attention in case anything went wrong. After this initial discussion, Matt noticed she was still hesitant so he suggested they hold an extra workshop with her. To this next workshop, Matt brought along one of his most talented pre-sales engineers, who did a deep dive demo with her, and spent a half-day answering the majority of her questions.

After additional meetings and several phone calls, Matt was delighted to hear her say, *"I'm excited we're going to do this."*
A few days later, the agreement was signed.

Lessons Learned:
Just one person can kill a deal, even with commitment from the C-level. Collaborating with the right people early in the process is crucial if you don't want deals to stall. Luckily, Matt had a strong sponsor (the CEO). Otherwise, the deal could very well have been handed over to his competitor.

Connect with Stakeholders on a Personal Level

Small things make a big difference when connecting with new people. Using social media like LinkedIn and Facebook and searching on Google can reveal lots of things you have in common with prospects. You can also dig up mutual contacts you have from social media.

Communicating about business related topics becomes a lot easier and more fun if you have mutual interests outside of work and can build rapport that way. Before meeting with new stakeholders many deal makers research what hobbies and interest they could have in common with them. Small facts about the person can also help: what kind of car they drive, what their education is or in which parts of the world they have lived.

Mutual Hobbies

A prospect that an account executive was meeting was an endurance athlete. He knew this based on the research he had done before the meeting. Normally the account execute wears a Rolex, but he put his sports watch on for this meeting as he also likes to do running and biking. In the meeting they were both wearing sports watches, which made it was easy to small talk and bond with the prospect in the meeting when they found out they have a similar hobby.

Mutual connections

An account executive was meeting a member of the management team of a prospect for the first time. The prospect asked him how well he knows the company. He answered by describing a few things he knew about their strategy, and added *"I also have a few friends working at your company"*. *"Oh yeah, who do you know?* -the prospect asked. He told them two names. One of them was in a high position within the company and they ended up talking about that person for a short while. The meeting went really smoothly. The mutual connection created trust between the two people that hadn't met each other before. Figuring out if they had mutual connections didn't require a lot of work.

Notes

Understanding the Customer's Ecosystem & External Stakeholders

Gone are the days of selling simple transactional products. Now, everything is becoming connected and intertwined. Whether someone is selling technology or hardware, the customer's supplier, partner and technology ecosystem is increasingly important to understand.

In the interviews, many deals were dependent on the deal maker's understanding of not only the customer's stakeholders (and their goals and challenges), but also the relevant organizations in the customer's ecosystem of partners and the relationships that the different stakeholders had with other partners.

Other partners and suppliers in the customer's ecosystem may be positive, neutral or hostile towards what you have to offer so make sure you get to know them and what they do.

All these different layers add complexity to deal making that modern deal makers must be able to identify and manage.

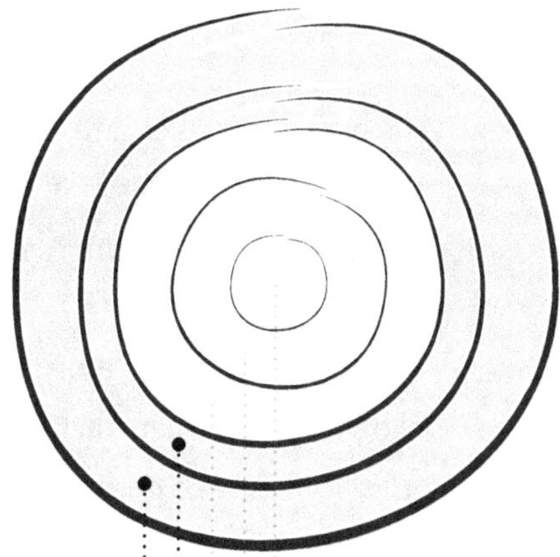

Leading Your Opportunity Team

Without a great team, deal makers cannot create the value that is needed to win competitive deals. Deal makers will also run out of time with all the different tasks that need to get done if they don't have a great team helping them.

The best deal makers are able to maintain a high-level vision of the opportunity while steering all the details of the sales project forward through their team, getting the team to engage with the customer's stakeholders.

The bigger the opportunity, the more you will be in trouble if you try to work alone. Nearly all of the deal makers that were interviewed highlighted the importance of teamwork in order to win large deals. Both technical experts and members of the management team were often engaging with the customer's stakeholders in the won deals that were analyzed.

"My role as account executive is to lead my team of experts. I'm in charge of doing what it takes to position us to win. This includes aligning and properly using our technical resources in the right way at each stage of the sales process and matching them with the right people on the customers side."

Notes

Preparing Your Team

One of the interviewed deal makers said he arms his team of experts with "fast facts" before important meetings, because he wants his experts to be better prepared than the competitors.

This deal maker said it's his responsibility to make sure his pre-sales experts are prepared for every important meeting. He said that even though they might miss some small details, his team never misses what is most important to the customer.

A few examples of the types of things to brief your team on:

- The CIO has said that moving to cloud to cut costs by 20% is his first priority, but he is worried about the cyber security risks of cheaper cloud solutions.

- The CFO said in the Q1 investor call that preserving cash is his #1 priority this year.

- The head of production wants to increase the planned maintenance percentage (PMP) from 75% to 90%.

Example of an Opportunity Team

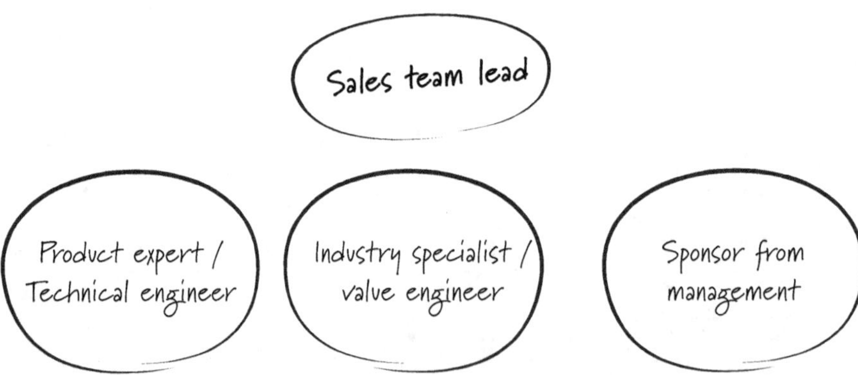

Notes

Using Your Team to Engage on Multiple Levels

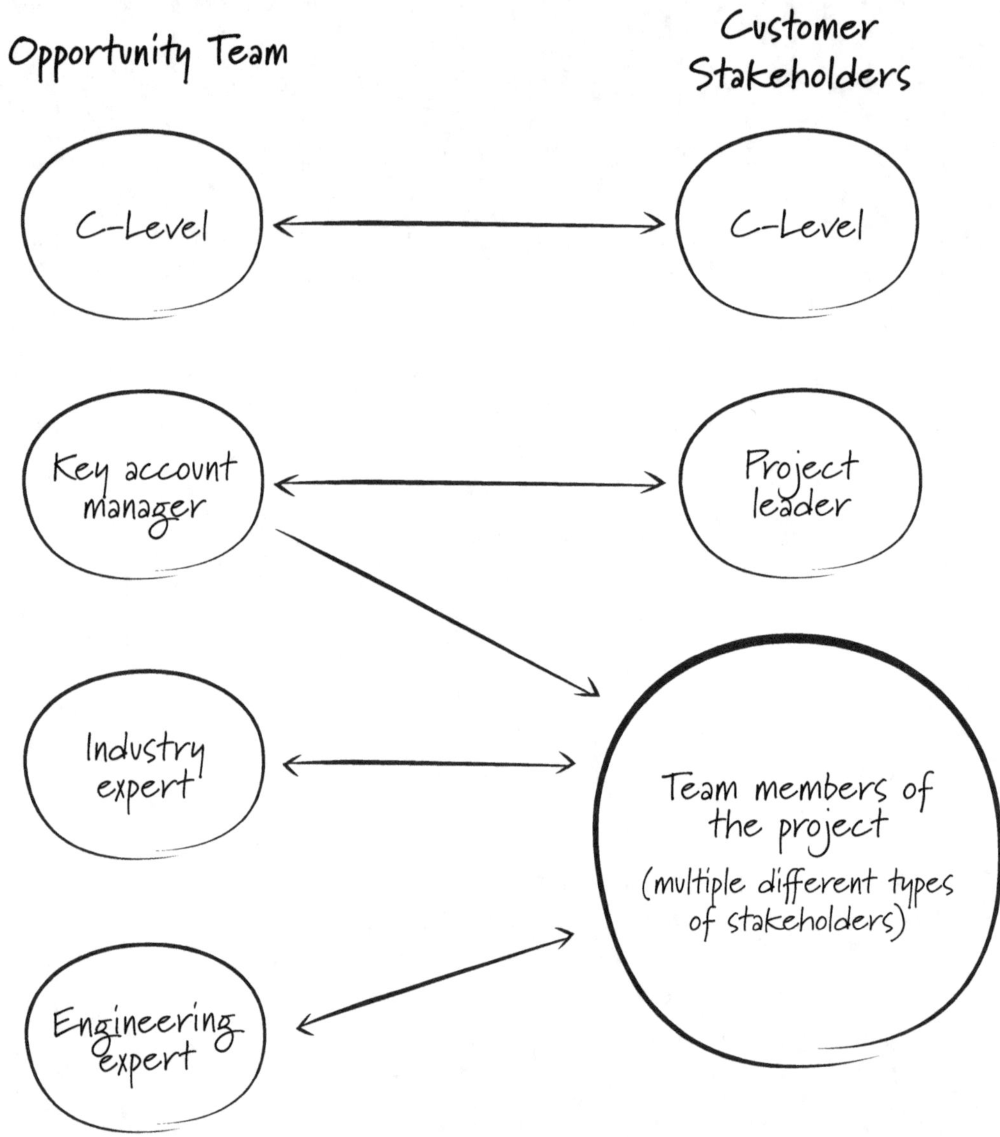

"Arianna," a key account manager for an engineering company, had a meeting with a project leader who was in charge of building a team that would arrange a bidding process to acquire consulting services to plan their new manufacturing production line.

Arianna knew she had good chances of winning this deal, because the opportunity was very early stage and there were still many months left before the official buying process would start. What she was worried about was that her main competitor also had a good relationship with this customer and if the competitor had their best resources allocated to this project, then the competitive situation would be very tough.

It turned out that the competitors were in fact able to get their best resources allocated to this project. Arianna knew that in order to win they would have to work even better as a team and engage the customer on a higher level than her primary point of contact.

Arianna met twice with the project leader, but after that she got her pre-sales resources with industry knowledge involved with the customer's experts. The project leader was one notch below the CEO in the organization. The decision for this project would eventually be made by the CEO. She knew that they had to succeed at engaging the C-level, because technically they would be very similar to the competitors. Although Arianna had met the customer's CEO once before, she knew that if she could leverage her companys CEO, they would more likely have good strategic level discussions. She was able to get her CEO interested in engaging with the customers CEO and they ended up having a few meetings together.

Arianna's team worked very smoothly with the project team from the beginning and the CEOs seemed to get along very well. In addition to this, Arianna's and the project leader's personalities also matched very well.

Eventually, they ended up winning the deal. Arianna believes the main reason they won the deal was because of their excellent engagement on every level. During the sales process they were able to add value on every stakeholder level.

Lessons Learned
Different stakeholders want to talk to people on their own level or above. Never underestimate the impact that personal chemistry can have.

Notes

Chapter 9

Business Value Discovery

"**Selling isn't about your product, it's about being curious of how you can improve your customer's business.**"

"Marty" started working for a company with new technology that no one was using yet. There weren't any use cases or references available at the time, but he was in charge of new business development, so it was his responsibility to jumpstart the business and get the first references. He was selling the ability to get internet connectivity to mobile devices at a time when it was still very rare (the 1990s).

A customer he was engaged with was interested, but when he heard what it would cost he quickly became uninterested, saying: *"Forget it...this is never going to happen."*

Another prospect that had a lot of service technicians was also slightly interested at first, but then they said that what he was selling was "science fiction" and the clear answer was, "No!". After this initial meeting, Marty looked into the numbers of the company, how their revenue and profits had developed and how many service technicians they had. Marty realized that even a slight increase in productivity could make a huge difference for this prospect.

Marty was able to get another meeting and he asked the prospect to forget all their earlier conversations and just give a new idea a chance. When they met, he asked:

> "Right now your field service engineers have to come back to the workshop multiple times per day for information about new work orders. What if they didn't need to come back for information? What could the impact be?"

The prospect promised to have someone look at the numbers. In the next meeting they told him they had worked on the numbers and they were very pleased with the potential impact. On average they counted out that they could potentially have their field service engineers do one more job per day, which was a huge improvement. Within weeks they had signed an agreement to do a pilot project, which turned out to be an enormous success. According to the deal maker, this was one of the first, if not the very first time a business used a mobile app in Europe.

This new customer ended up becoming their most important reference and a crucial stepping stone to developing this business to the next level. This wasn't how Marty had imagined customers would use the technology, but he had found a common problem that many companies experienced, and there was substantial value in solving this problem.

Notes

"You have to assume on every deal that your competitor has a very similar product. You can talk product value until you are blue in the face, but the difference between winning and losing is less about product, and more about how well you understand the various variables, dynamics and hidden agendas that people have and really understanding what is important to them."

Notes

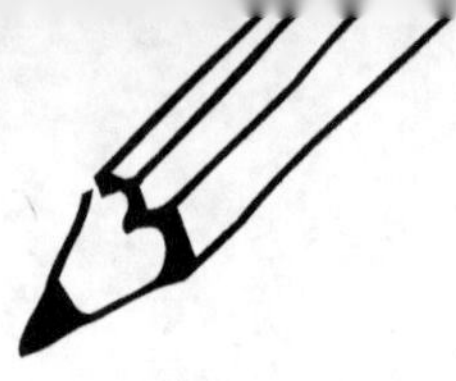

Discovery Creates Value

Discovery done right creates value for all the different stakeholders. Discovery is something deal makers typically do in all meetings and calls, because they are constantly uncovering information. In complex deals there is so much information and so many stakeholders that there needs to be a formal discovery process to be able to efficiently gather information, educate the stakeholders and position the solution to fit the different stakeholder needs.

Discovery typically happens between recognizing that there is potential for cooperation and creating a proposal or demonstration. In the interviews it became very clear that the best discovery creates a bond between the stakeholders and the deal makers team because together they learn new things. The educational aspect of Discovery was a large reason why deal makers believe they were able to gain the trust of key stakeholders and win important deals. The next pages will help you structure your own discovery approach so you can create value for the multiple stakeholders you need to engage.

"Make discovery personal, make it relevant, make it interesting."

Heavy vs Light Discovery

Busy stakeholders higher up in organizations will hesitate spending time on issues that aren't absolutely critical. The benefits must be very compelling for the customer to spend time doing deeper discovery together with a potential vendor.

In this section, there are ideas that can be implemented both for a lighter and heavier discovery approach. A light discovery may consist of a few interviews that are then analyzed and reported back in the next meeting. A heavier approach would be workshops that can take hours, days—even weeks. Sometimes discovery includes site visits or lab testing, as well as a series of interviews and data analysis. Most often it's pre-sales or some type of subject matter/domain expert that conducts the discovery, but in some instances, especially in lighter discovery, the deal maker facilitates the sessions.

Discovery should be so valuable that customers would even in some cases be willing to pay for it, if the vendor didn't provide it for free. In opportunities that score poorly on the qualification matrix, one option is to have the customer pay for the diagnosis of their needs (discovery).

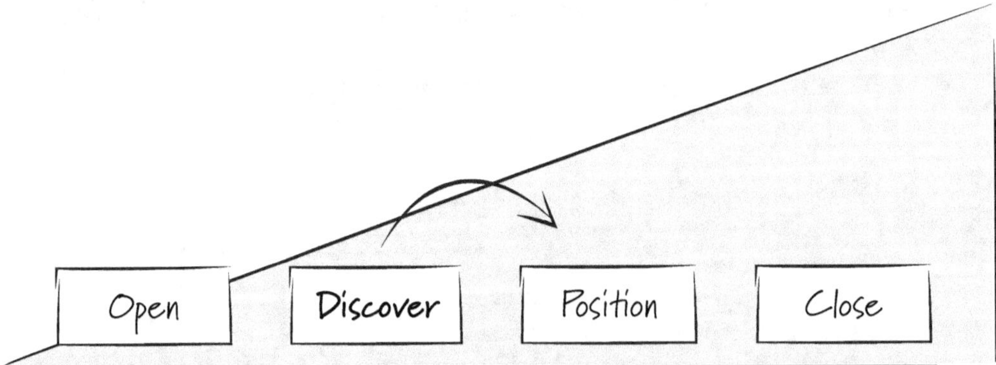

Many of the interviewed deal makers had some kind of official discovery concept that included gathering data, information and points of views of the different stakeholders. A few names for discovery concepts that came up in the interviews were:

- **Business discovery workshop**
- **Pre-study**
- **Audit**
- **Business Value realization**
- **Maturity assessment**
- **Value management**
- **Visioning workshop**

Notes

....

....

....

....

....

....

Success Requires Discovery on Two Levels

89% of B2B buyers state that the vendors they've bought from made it easier to show ROI and/or build a business case for the purchase" [1]

71% of sales leaders say their salespeople fail to connect their solutions to clients' business needs [2]

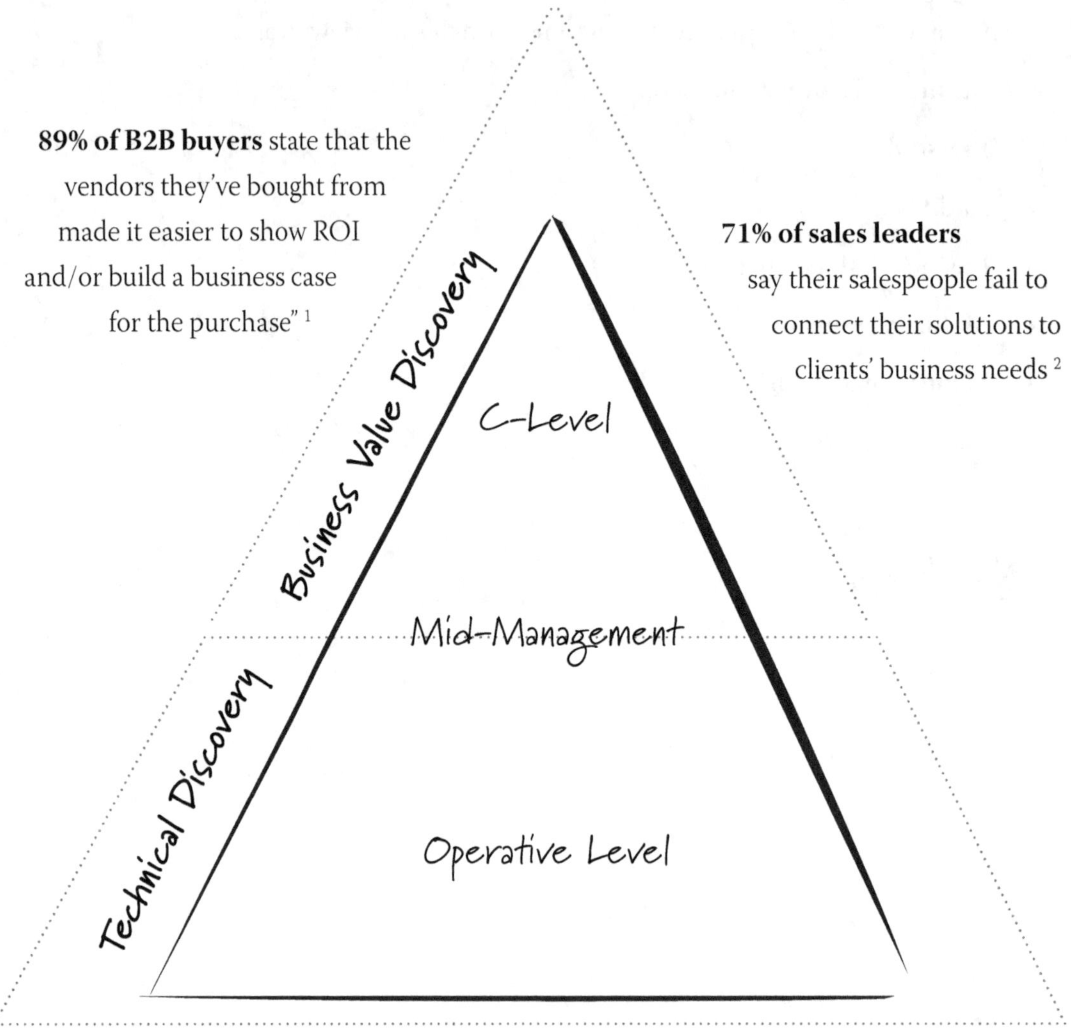

The bigger the investment, the more likely it is that the decision will be made on higher levels within the organization. Many interviewed deal makers talked about "technical wins" and "business wins". Their main point was that it's not enough to get a technical win, because business leaders don't care about the technology or the specifications. They care about business results. Commercial justification is done with the customers figures. Benchmark data can be used, but the justification should always be done with the customer's validated business numbers. If there are no numbers in the deal maker's presentations and proposals, then there is no financial justification.

In this section we focus on succeeding in the 'Business Value Discovery', because this is the more challenging and based on the interviews, it's also more important.

Notes

Why is Discovery Important?

We're living in a global and highly competitive world. Products and technology are already commoditized beyond what vendors think. Customers look at different solutions that can solve their problems, but they all look very similar.

It's the deal makers and their teams that differentiate the solutions based on the customer's specific needs. Those who are able to identify problems and their impacts on multiple levels, as well as tie them to the customer's strategy, will put themselves in the best position to win.

"I don't sell software.
I sell business results that
are achieved by improving
the customer's crucial
business processes."

Discovery Topics

Results
Ultimately you are selling results, not your solution. Find out what the financial objectives are that need to be reached.

Problems
Explore what problems now or in the future will stop them from reaching their financial objectives.

Solution
Find the best option to solve their problems and achieve results. The solution is merely a bridge for achieving their desired results.

What We Need to Find Out in Discovery

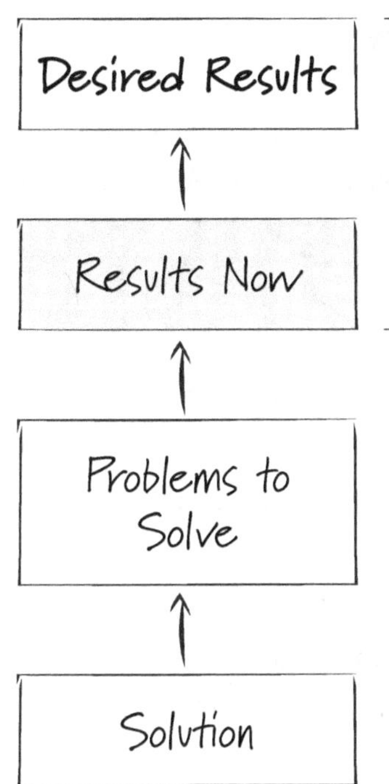

How big is the gap between where they are and where they want to be?

Without knowing the gap, we will never be able to know how big of an investment can be justified to solve the problems.

How serious are their problems?
What happens if the problems go unsolved?

Finding a "Good Enough" Solution for Multiple Stakeholders

Every large purchase has its pros and cons, and there will never be any perfect decisions. The goal is to position the solution to help each of the stakeholders achieve their objectives while minimizing risks.

Understanding levels 1 and 2 are critical in order to take everyone's points of view into consideration and be able to gain group consensus on what the problems are and how these problems link to each other. There will be conflicts and differences between stakeholders, but the goal is to find common ground and balance their different needs.

Only when the stakeholders have a joint point of view on the problems will there be a chance to agree on what the right solution is. The chosen solution is hardly ever perfect, but good enough to satisfy the needs of multiple stakeholders.

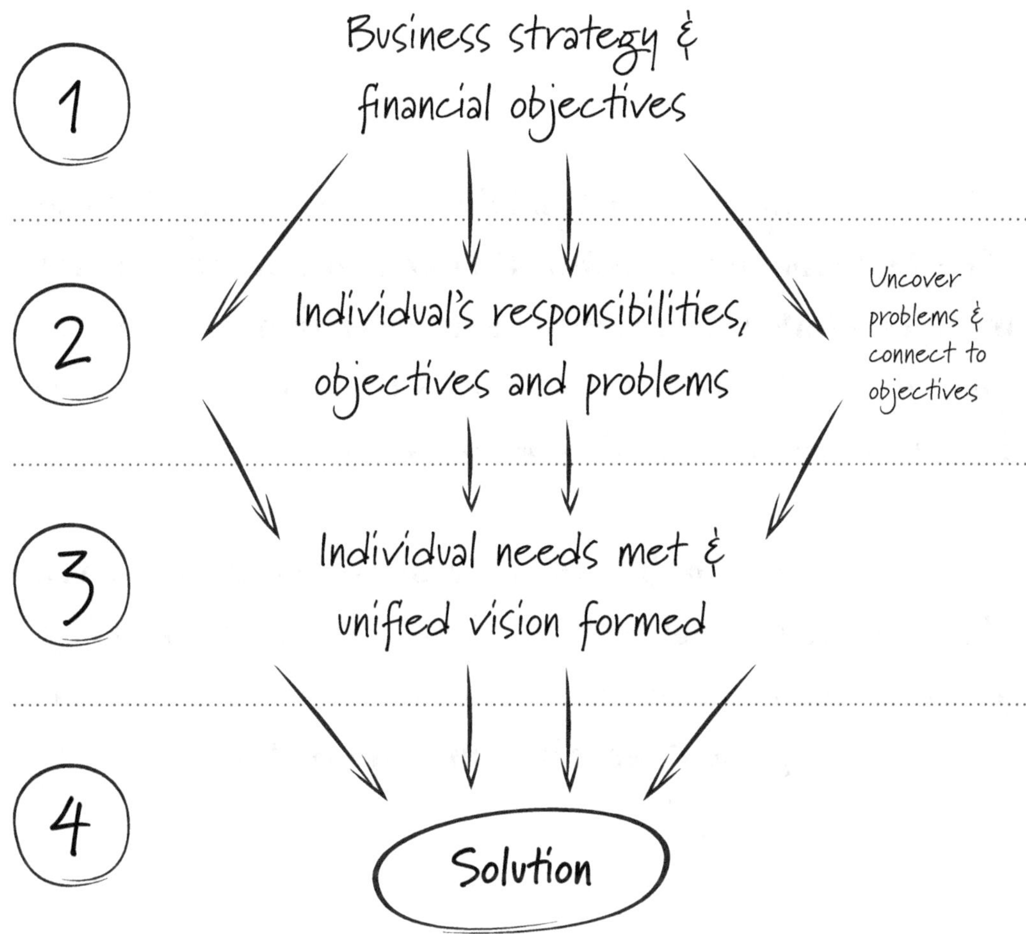

1
Business strategy & financial objectives
2
Individual's responsibilities, objectives and problems
Uncover problems & connect to objectives
3
Individual needs met & unified vision formed
4
Solution

"Customers operate in silos, blindly unaware of what the other departments are doing. If I don't do a broad discovery with stakeholders from different departments, then each department will buy point-solutions that don't bring synergies and increased overall benefits for the whole company."

"When I understand the broad picture by working with the different departments, I can create more value with our solutions and bring business synergies that the customer's management team becomes interested in."

Different Stakeholders Often Require Unique Approaches

"John," an account executive focused on finding new clients, had been talking with Anna, the head of the procurement department, about replacing an IT-solution that the whole company was using. Anna reported directly to a person in the management team, in an organization with over 50,000 employees.

Anna believed they could save money by improving a few of their important business processes and after some talks with John, she believed his solution could be the difference maker for their global organization. Their existing solution would have required an upgrade to get the necessary features, but Anna was not convinced that this would be the best option for them.

> "It felt like there were three different sales processes simultaneously in play with the same opportunity."

This new system would be touching multiple departments. The heads of two other departments (finance and IT) were also involved, and together these three people formed the primary stakeholder group, that would make the decision. If any of them opposed the deal and wanted to stick to the old solution, he would not have good chances of winning.

These three different stakeholders were completely different in backgrounds and personalities and they also had very different business objectives. Anna was innovative and a very dominating personality, the second stakeholder feared the risk in changing vendors and didn't understand the technology and the third was very shy, conservative and worried about operational details. John noticed that one of these stakeholders didn't speak out and talk about her true fears when the others were with her in the same meetings. John realized that in order to fully understand these three stakeholders and cooperate with them he would have to approach them in very different ways. John often held meetings and presentations separately with the different stakeholders until he fully understood each of them. This approach paid off as he was eventually able to win this deal, which ended up being the biggest deal of the year for him, and actually the biggest John's entire company won that year.

Lessons Learned

Afterwards, John realized that he had been working on this opportunity with three three different sales processes simultaneously. Without this approach, he doesn't believe he would have won this deal.

Uncovering Immediate vs. Future Needs in Discovery

Small problems that can be fixed immediately, typically lead to small and quick deals. Large problems and large potential problems lead to bigger investments.

Asking strategic questions about goals, needs and risks, and using insights about the industry trends and future developments is often needed for identifying bigger deals. The deal maker needs to be able to get the customer to evaluate how their current problems will impact their future success. This means getting the customer to look into the future and force them to take a stance on potential problems they'll face if they do not invest now.

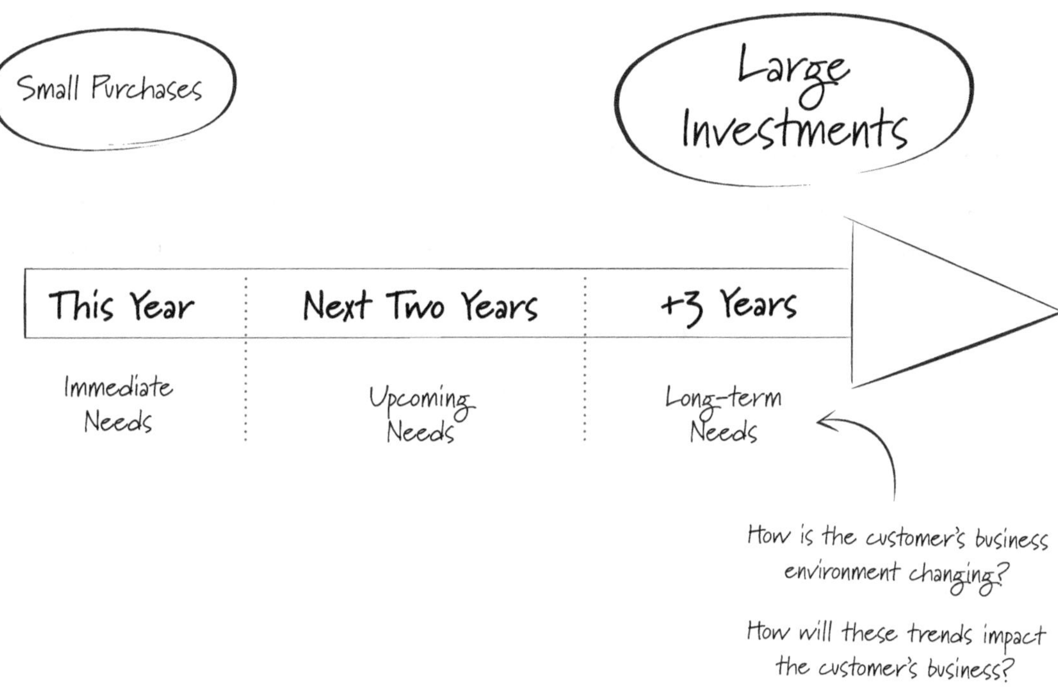

Discovery Tips From the Pro's

Don't Talk about Your Own Product Too Early

Discuss their business issues and share your insights about what other companies are doing.

Avoid Interrogation

Discovery is supposed to be a pleasant conversation and both parties need to get value out of the discussion. Base your questions on the customers maturity.

Validate and Verify

Constantly validate your findings with the right stakeholders to make sure you are on the right track.

Give the Prospect Context When You Ask Questions

Guide with insights & use cases or references when asking questions to give the person solid context to understand what you are looking to hear before you present your question.

For example:

"Typically in your industry, the manufacturing cycle time is 16 days, where are you at right now?"

This is a better way of asking as opposed to:

"What is your manufacturing cycle time?"

Challenge, But Don't Be Too Obvious

To make an impact, you must often be able to challenge customers, but in a way that lets the customer come up with their own conclusions. You cannot be so obvious when you challenge (using questions with context help with this).

Drill Deep

You need to get to the root causes of their problems that they may or may not have considered before. WHY is the most powerful word you can use. Using why to probe and dig deeper into the problems is a simple and powerful way to get to the root cause.

Probe for implications (both negative and positive)

- *What is the total impact of the problems you've described?*

- *What happens if you don't succeed? Will you lose profits? Will your competitors steal your market share?*

- *What happens if you stay the same?*

- *If you succeed at solving this problem, what will it help you achieve?*

Discovery Content –
Examples of Things to Find Out

Changes in the market and business environment?

Changes in the company's strategy?

Changes in the company's financial results & goals?

What will stop them from succeeding?

What happens if they don't solve their problems?

Does the customer understand what is really causing their problems?

How have they already tried to solve their problems?

Why haven't their attempts to solve the problems succeeded?

What are the metrics that will be used to measure success?

What is their current solution and what other options are they looking at?

These are examples of how a deal maker asked questions in a light discovery meeting that was booked after the deal maker received a qualified lead from a business development rep.

Uncovered why the customer was now interested:

"What has changed, since you haven't had a solution earlier, and are now looking at buying a solution?"

Probed where their business was heading:

"In your industry, most companies are growing service revenues by 20-30% per year. What is your service revenue trend?"

Justified why he was asking certain questions:

"The reason why I'm asking that is that I talk to many companies who are trying to improve their service organizations profit, by eliminating unnecessary customer visits ... are you pursuing that?

Painted a scenario for the customer and asked to take a stance:

"The service person visits the site to fix something. Then the customer asks, "could you look at this other machine that has been having problems"? Does this happen to your service engineers?"

Qualified and started a conversation to create a mutual action plan:

"Assuming a good fit with financial benefits, and a good demo and presentation, what would lead to us being selected?"

Incorporate "mini-stories" into your discovery that give context and make answering questions easier:

Discovery Should Educate the Customer

The goal is to help us understand the customer's situation better, but also to help the customer understand their own situation and their opportunities for improvement better:

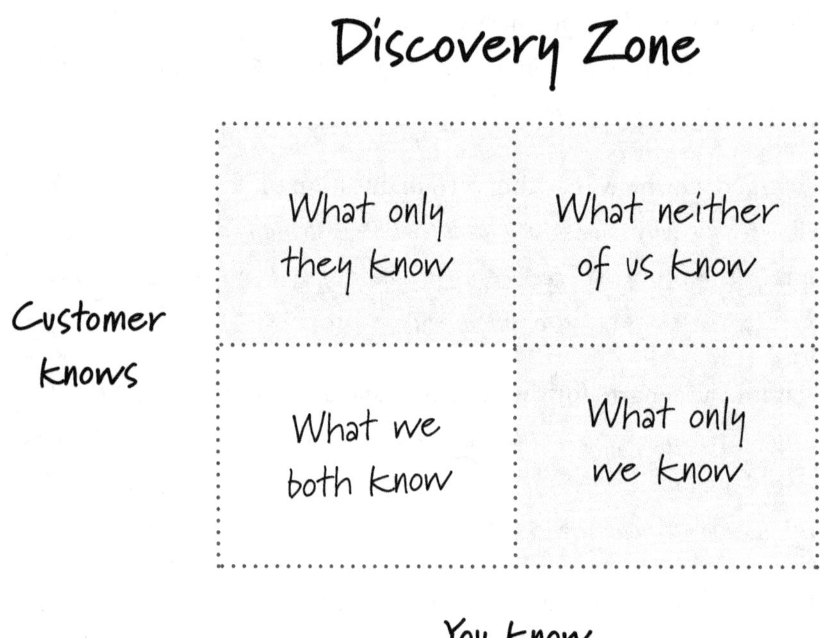

A teleoperator needed a small security assessment for an application related to their billing process. A cyber security partner of theirs was invited to discuss this project with them because the customer knew they had a simple solution for this.

In the meeting the cyber security company's senior account executive, "Joseph," (or Joe as he likes to be called), requested that they look at how this specific process is connected to the other IT platforms being used, so he asked if they had a picture of the entire architecture. They found a blueprint of the IT-architecture, which included servers, components, firewalls, etc.. The whole architecture couldn't fit on one screen, because it was so large. As they looked at this picture, Joe asked more questions. Joe asked them to describe the process by suggesting they explain how their end-to-end billing process works as well as which different processes are linked to it.

During the end-to-end explanation, Joe asked questions like, *"What triggers the information to move and what systems does it move to? Who maintains and who has access to the different systems?"*

> The account executive truly wanted to help the customer. This approach led to a solution being selected that was ten times larger than the customer originally thought they needed.

This broader approach allowed Joe to move the discussion from technical issues, to business impact. There were so many things they had to cover, that they booked a separate workshop. In this next workshop, instead of just doing discovery about their IT-environment, Joe was able to understand the key business processes that would be impacted. For the first time, he was finally able to uncover the full scope of potential risks that the client was exposing themselves to.

The customer learned a great deal through the discussions and Joe potentially saved the client from massive security problems later. Because he didn't want to make a quick sale and truly wanted to help the customer, Joe was able to get the customer to make an investment that was ten times larger than the customer had originally thought they needed.

Lessons Learned

The customer can often pinpoint specific problems, but sometimes they need someone from the outside to help see the big picture. A seller who helps the customer see the big picture often creates a so-called "value gap" between what the customer thinks they need and what they really need.

Educational Discovery

An automotive manufacturer was having problems with one major feature of their infotainment system, and it was clearly impacting the driving experience for their customers. They had received some bad reviews and were desperate to fix the problem, which meant finding a new vendor to replace the old one.

They sent an RFP to 15 different vendors that could deliver the type of technology they were looking for.

"Phil," a sales director, had met with this company about a half year before they proactively started contacting vendors, because he had heard that they were getting negative feedback from customers. At that time the automotive manufacturer had not yet fully understood the seriousness of the problem higher up in the organization and were not ready to do anything about the problems yet.

> The prospect had no way of making a decision when they didn't understand enough about what they were buying.

Now, half a year later, procurement was in charge of finding a new vendor and Phil was invited to present a proposal to the engineers, the infotainment product manager and quality assurance team. They wanted to find "the best provider" in the market so they don't face these problems ever again. But Phil's team realized that the customer wasn't experienced enough to know how to evaluate what the "best" is.

Phil identified that one of the reasons they may have been in trouble in the first place was the lack of knowledge in the specific technology to begin with. The prospect had no way of making the best decision when they didn't understand enough about what they were looking to buy.

To Phil, it was clear that they didn't have the right type of "quality metrics" that they would need to verify and compare the quality of the different options. Together with the help of Phil's pre-sales experts they created the right quality metrics for the auto manufacturer and based on these metrics they started testing the quality of the different technologies. Phil knew at this point that an immense amount of trust had been created since they started using the quality metrics established together with Phil's team. The sales process lasted nearly a year, and Phil was more of a project manager in this phase, because there were so many different stakeholders and "tracks" as he called them, to manage. Eventually Phil and his team won this deal.

Lessons Learned

Once the agreement was signed the engineers and quality assurance personnel told Phil and his colleagues that they had learned things from them that they hadn't learned from other vendors. The vendor that educates customers is often perceived as the most trustworthy partner when making critical decisions.

Identifying a Win-Theme

The goal is to differentiate you from other options by aligning what you're offering with the customer's strategy and goals in a clearer way than other vendors.

Once you've gained a good understanding of the issues at hand, you can craft a win-theme. The win-theme becomes the main message that is always brought up in all conversations with the customer and it's the reason you are working on this deal with your team. The win-theme is typically a combination of results and benefits that positions you for the win and can later become a slogan or one-liner that defines the mission of the deal.

For Example:

- "Cut costs without downsizing Your workforce!"
- "Increase efficiency on a global scale with a mobile first organization!"
- "Increase workforce productivity by improving user-experiences in online meetings."

Many deal makers emphasized the importance of consistency in communicating the win-theme because it can become forgotten when there are so many different stakeholders involved in the long sales process. What makes communicating a win-theme difficult in complex deals is that it often has slight differences depending on the stakeholder you are communicating with.

"If our story is not strong and consistent, no one will remember it."

"Manuel," a technology sales executive, had met the CEO of a service company that boasted a strong profit margin. The two main owners of the company had been quite satisfied with the business for a long time, but they were now at a crossroads. The owners realized they had to make a decision about whether they should grow the business or keep it as a small "lifestyle" business that churns a nice annual profit. The strong market favored expansion. The right time to make decisions about their future was now. If they wanted to grow they would need to put in place systems and processes that made it possible to manage growth. The existing business set-up was not adequate for scaling the business up and neither of the owners had scaled up a business before.

Manuel entered into discussions with the company when they were analyzing what kind of solutions could help them scale their service business. Even though they were analyzing different solutions, they weren't necessarily going to buy anything unless they decided to scale up the business. Now, they were just building the plan for scaling. Manuel's technology could serve as the backbone in the background that would make it possible to plan and manage the growing amount of people delivering the service to customers.

Earlier they weren't sure how to scale up the business, and that was one of the reasons they had never seriously considered expansion as a viable option. But with the help of Manuel, they could more clearly see how it could be done. The technology Manuel was selling was a great fit, but the fit didn't matter unless the owners made a simple but tough decision.

It all ended up coming down to whether or not the owners and their management team wanted to scale the business or remain a small lifestyle business. This became the win-theme Manuel started using in every encounter with them.

With a clear roadmap, strategy and trust of how the plans would be executed to scaling the business, the owners finally made the sizable investment of scaling up the company. There were still significant risks involved, but they felt confident enough in the solution Manuel was selling.

> Scale the business or remain a small lifestyle business?

They became an important partner to Manuel's company. So important, that they were even developing features together for upcoming software releases.

Lessons Learned

Ultimately, Manuel wasn't selling technology, but instead, was focused on helping them envision and plan how they would transform their business, taking it to a whole new level.

Heavy Qualification

Compared to the qualification after your first meeting(s), the qualification going forward will have to be more detail oriented to avoid wasting further time if the chance of winning the deal are low. The sales process for complex deals remains resource-intensive as you move forward,
so it makes sense to analyze if you should progress in the sales process.

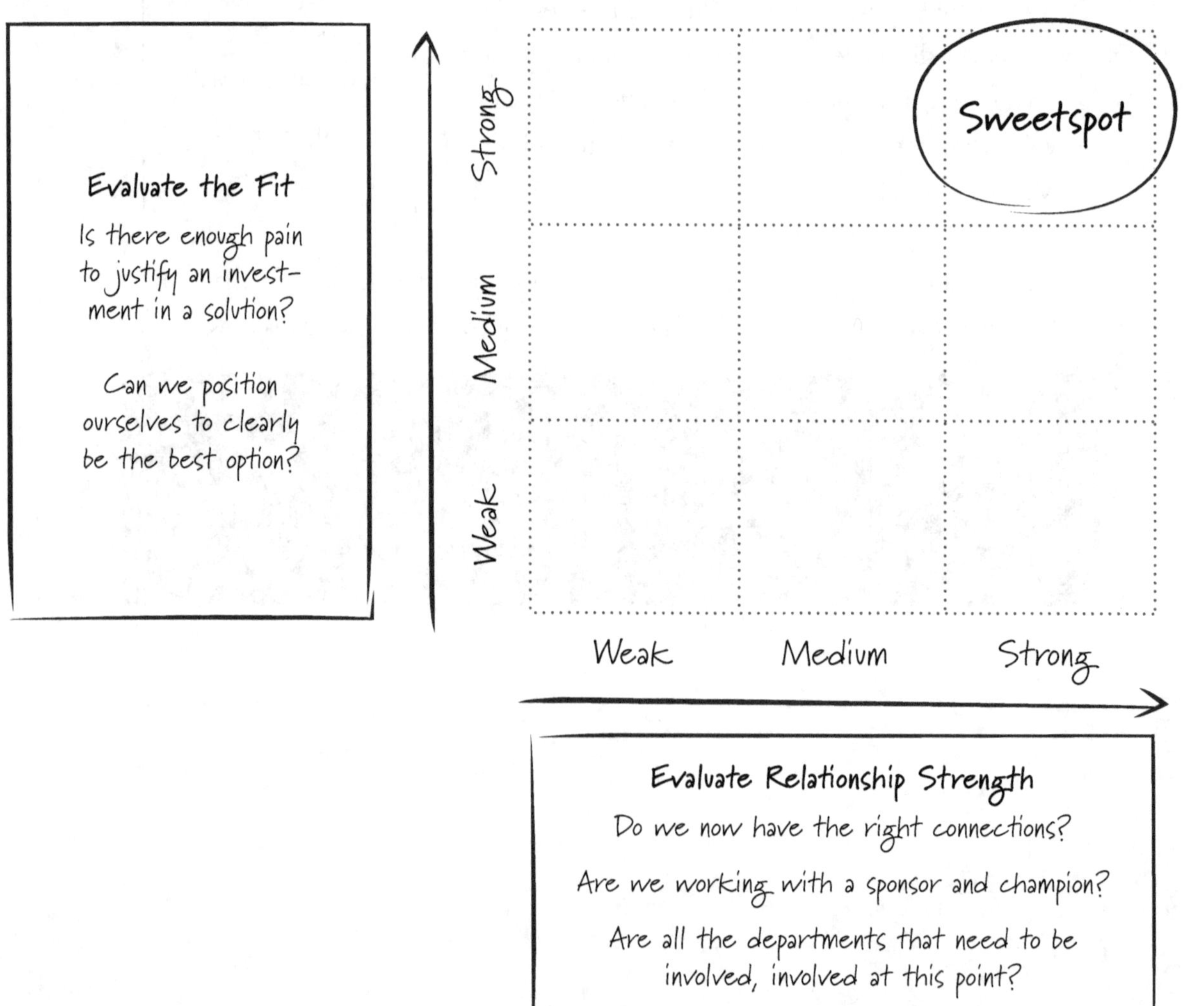

Other Heavy Qualification Questions

- What is the criteria at this point for making the decision?
- What are their technical / functional requirements?
- Does our portfolio have a match with their needs?
- Do we have suitable references with results?
- Can we differentiate from other options?
- Has the customer already tried fixing these problems?
- Is there a risk they may try solving their problems in an alternative way?

WHEN

- Is there a set timeframe for when results need to be achieved?
- Is there a set timeframe for the purchase decision?
- What is the compelling event that forces them to make decision?

HOW

- Do they have the necessary resources to invest?
- Will other projects or investments have to be deprioritized in order to make this investment?
- Is it clear how and who will fund the project?

Lack of Proper Qualification Can Lead to Bitter Losses

A pulp and paper manufacturer realized it would need to upgrade its surveillance systems. Earlier, they'd chosen site-specific systems for their different manufacturing locations. Now, they wanted to have the same technology used in all their facilities so that they could streamline the way they manage the security of their facilities.

A sales manager named "Erik" and his team did a quick analysis and learned they could provide the customer with the technology they were looking for. Erik visited several sites and created documentation surrounding the company's technical needs. The customer hadn't yet established their official project team as this wasn't an official project just yet. Erik's team estimated the lifecycle costs of switching over to new technology and evaluated what the customer's options were. They had different types of planning meetings and at some point this became an official project with a project manager and a team. The key contact they had been working with from the beginning was the project manager. Erik's team even built a big part of the RFP that they would send to other vendors. At this point, procurement stepped in and the nature of the collaboration took a turn. The contact in procurement didn't want to cooperate with Erik.

> The sales manager realized him and his team had been used for "free consultation" for several years

All along, Erik assumed that the project manager (who was fairly high up in the organization) and a few other business stakeholders, would be making the final decision. This is what typically happened with the deals Erik worked on. Erik was sure that since the collaboration went so well with the project manager (his champion...or so he thought) that they had very high chances of winning the deal. When procurement stepped in to evaluate the vendors, the project team disappeared and stopped communicating with them. A procurement person, whom they had never met before stepped in and started leading the project. Little by little, Erik learned that in this organization procurement had much more political power than the typical customers he worked with. The stakeholders he had been engaged with had very little political power in terms of the final decision.

Erik realized he and his team had been used for what was essentially a "free consultation" before procurement stepped in. Erik estimates that the cost of all the work they did was around 70.000€. Procurement ended up cutting out and changing a few of the specifications, choosing the cheaper alternative—which wasn't Erik's. Erik later heard that the project manager got a lot of praise for managing the project so well. Ouch. That stings!

Lessons Learned

The qualification was way too light before starting the resource-intensive sales process. Erik realized that even though their technology was the best of all the options, the value they could create with their solutions was in fact much higher in other verticals, not in the pulp and paper industry. The customer chose a "good enough" solution that covered most of their needs. Erik didn't understand the customer's official buying process and who really held the political power within the company. In retrospect, if Erik had known how this company operated, he would have sold a consultation project in the beginning instead of doing the pre-sales work for free.

Working with Your Champion as You Move to the Position Stage

Many elements of the opportunity plan are used in the mutual action plan created together with the champion or sponsor. The acronym M. A. P. stands for the "mutual action plan." The action plan is literally a map of how you will reach the final destination together. The plan should be created by working backwards from the results customers wants to achieve. You risk failure if you don't create the M. A. P. with the customer.

Creating the M. A. P. is a great qualification exercise. If your champion truly wants you to win, they will gladly work on the plan together.

To create a solid mutual action plan, focus on buying first, selling second!

The plan should answer this question:

What needs to happen within the buyer's organization to move the deal forward?

Mutual Action Plan
Content Ideas

Strategy & financial targets

Objectives & business issues that must be solved

The outcome that this solution/project will achieve

Risk or cost of inaction or project delays

Who are the key people that need to be involved from the customer's side and from the vendor's side

Buying process (unofficial and official)

Possible roadblocks

Timeline of key milestones with tasks, dates and attendees:
1. Discovery meetings
2. Technical approval
3. Proposal review with project team
4. Proposal accepted in management meeting
5. Legal and contracts
6. Agreement signed
7. Implementation started
8. Project implementation complete
9. Results

Checklist

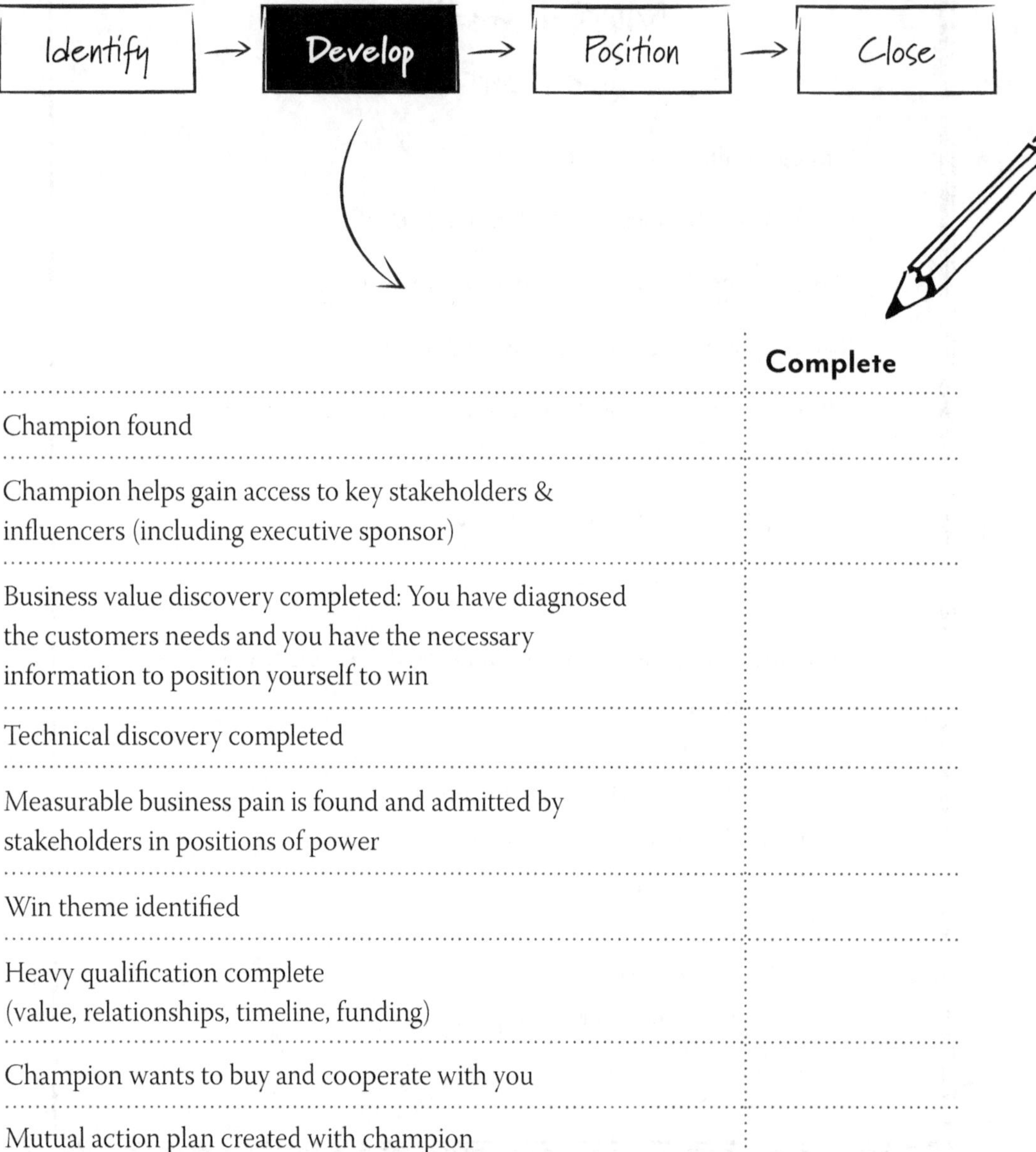

	Complete
Champion found	
Champion helps gain access to key stakeholders & influencers (including executive sponsor)	
Business value discovery completed: You have diagnosed the customers needs and you have the necessary information to position yourself to win	
Technical discovery completed	
Measurable business pain is found and admitted by stakeholders in positions of power	
Win theme identified	
Heavy qualification complete (value, relationships, timeline, funding)	
Champion wants to buy and cooperate with you	
Mutual action plan created with champion	

PART III

Positioning Yourself to Win

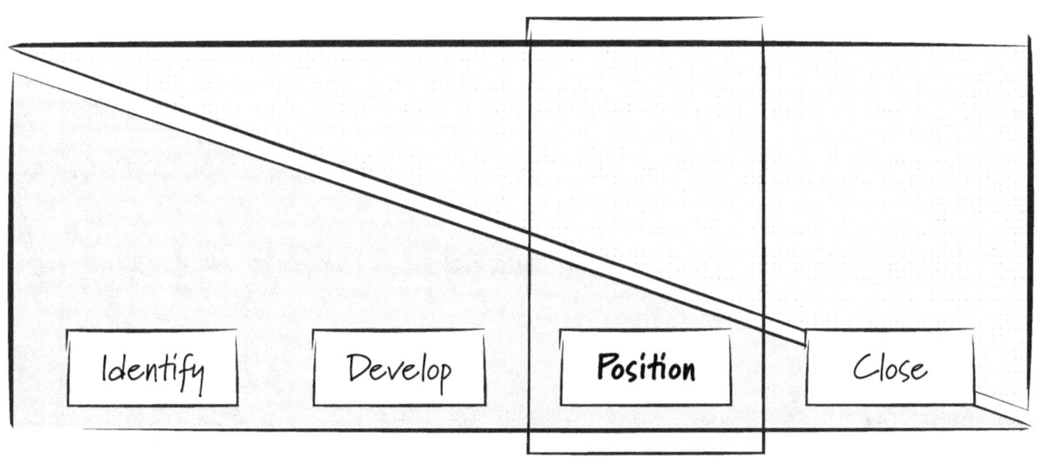

Goals in This Stage

Gain acceptance from the customer that you understand their problems & how those problems impact their business

Connect the findings from discovery with your solution

Craft the proposal and case for change together with the customer (co-create the solution and approach for best results)

Position your value with key stakeholders before discussing pricing

Get acceptance that your solution is the best option

Gain commitment to buy before entering contract negotiations

Evaluate Your Deal Making Habits

How do you get key stakeholders to validate your findings are accurate before presenting your proposal?

Do you typically find out which stakeholders prefer your competitors before you present your proposal?

When you move into the position stage do you usually have a strong champion you are working with?

Do you usually have a plan in place before you enter into negotiations?

Notes

Chapter 10

Confirm Your Findings and Align Your Solution

Confirm Findings Before Presenting the Solution

At this stage we want to diagnose the situation properly before presenting our solution. And, the situation is not properly diagnosed until we get the different stakeholders to confirm our findings. In so doing, they also confirm that we've understood their objectives correctly.

The goal is to get a consensus from different stakeholders on the issues and problems found during discovery. Based on this unified view, it's much easier to reach an understanding on the right solution.

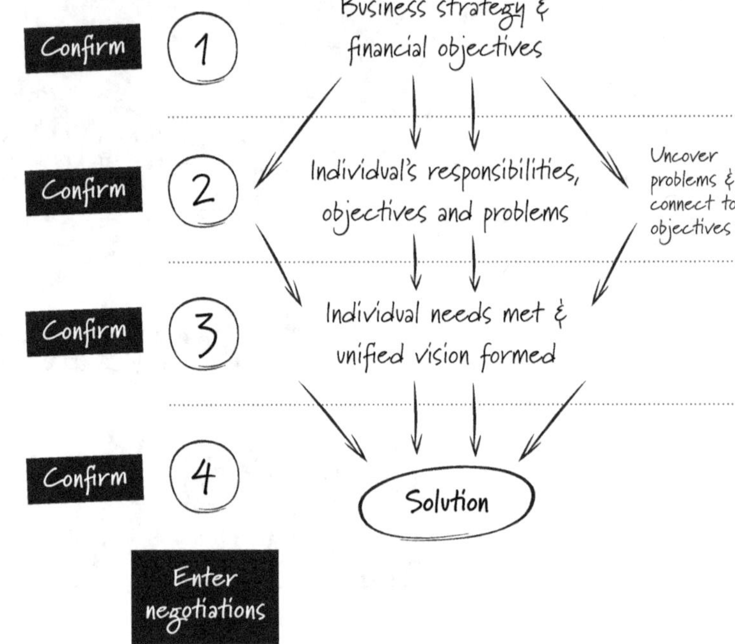

The solution presentation should tie everything together and help guide the discussions toward reaching a group consensus on what the right solution actually is.

The findings and information being presented should be so important that high level executives also attend the meetings. The key here is to avoid negotiating pricing and terms before the complete value of your solution is fully understood. Once it is, the different stakeholders will want to buy your solution.

Building Up the Perception of Value

With the help of a proper discovery, you are able to build as high of a perception of value as possible for different stakeholders that are influencing the overall purchase decision. The information you uncover in discovery should be used to stack up the value your solution can create for the customer's business. Different stakeholders will have different points of view of what is valuable and what is not. That's why it's so important to engage all stakeholders properly during discovery.

The benefits can come from multiple different things. The goal is to maximize the financial value on the left side of the scale. If the features of solutions with different price levels are somewhat the same, it makes it extremely hard for the customer to justify paying a premium price if there is not a compelling difference in value between the solutions. Each stakeholder has their own perception of what is valuable for the company and for them personally. They have their personal goals and dreams to achieve.

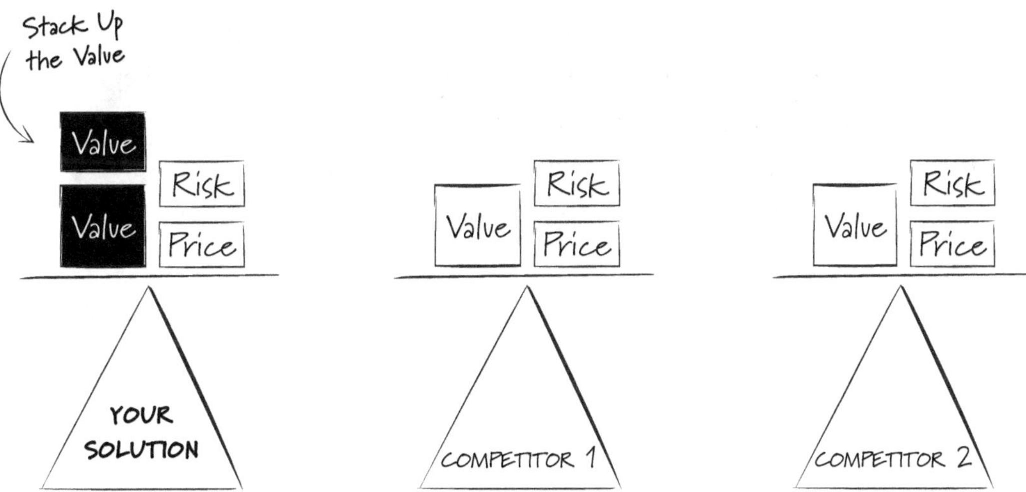

Gaining Commitment from Important Stakeholders

A company with several factories had serious challenges with their profit margin, which seemed to be mainly due to their higher than industry-average manufacturing costs. The management team wanted this to get solved one way or another. "Anthony," the account executive of a factory personnel outsourcing company, and his team were given access to different production sites to do an evaluation of their current situation. In order to succeed, they would have to make difficult decisions and potentially downsize their workforce, but this was a must if they wanted to keep the factories operating and at least save a majority of the jobs.

> They decided they would personally review the evaluation results with each plant manager before presenting to the management team.

Once the evaluation was complete, Anthony and his team were given the opportunity to present their findings to the management team and plant managers at the same time. However, they decided this would be too risky because they didn't have enough buy-in from the plant managers at this point yet. Anthony decided to personally review the evaluation results and plans with each plant manager first, then, he and his team would make their presentation. Making sure the plant managers did not feel threatened was a priority.

Anthony also understood that the management team would want to get the plant managers' feedback before making a decision. Secondly, once the implementation started, without a strong level of cooperation from plant managers, the plan would likely fail.

Anthony and his team used the same presentation they typically made to the management team, but in the findings, they focused on the specific factory that an individual plant manager was in charge of. They covered topics such as:

- What metrics they would be using to measure production efficiency
- How they would develop the maintenance of the production facilities
- Plans for reducing employees
- Annual plans for the coming years
- How to manage the change

Anthony ensured that the plant managers understood his solution and were committed to the proposed changes before moving forward with gaining commitment from the management team. The plant managers knew they would have to face painful changes, but now with Anthony and his team as their partner, they could save the future of their factories, as well as their own jobs. Within a few weeks of presenting to the management team, Anthony and the customer began working on the contract, which was eventually signed.

> **Lessons Learned**
> Extra focus on the plant managers helped ensure no one stalled or sabotaged the deal. Typically, plant managers have acted as roadblocks in similar cases. The implementation went smoothly because the plant managers' commitment was gained in advance.

Aligning Your Solution with the Customer's Strategy

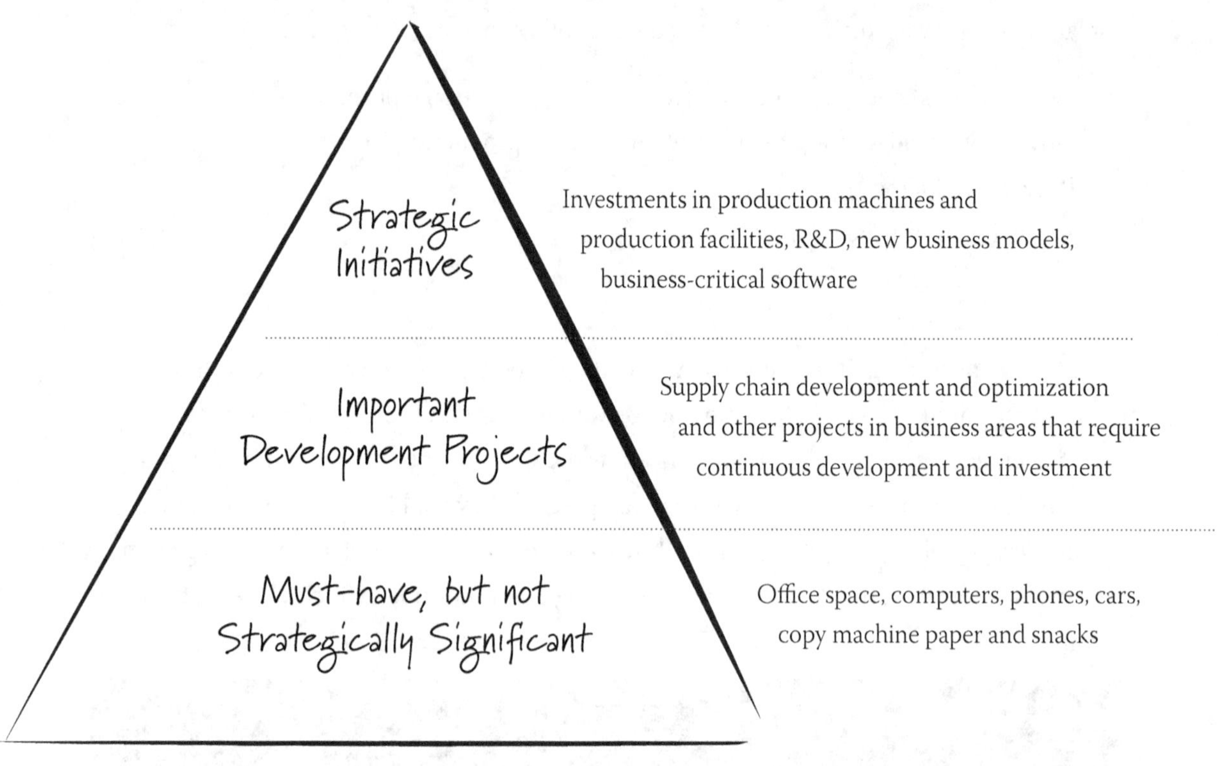

Since your value and differentiation doesn't come from your solution, you cannot position the value of your solution unless you link it to the customer's measurable business objectives and critical problems.

The closer you can position yourself to business-critical processes and strategically important initiatives, the more likely it is your project will get funding. This is especially important if you've created the demand to buy. However, if this is an unplanned purchase, priorities may have to shift.

Larger purchases have to be aligned with the customer's strategic initiatives.

Notes

Aligning with Strategic Initiatives

"Martin," a sales manager of heavy machinery, was able to book a call with a manager from one of his most important prospect accounts. The manager was a few levels below the main management team, but he had a good handle on their manufacturing strategy. Martin learned that they had recently changed their strategy and wanted to increase profitability.

One initiative that the prospect wanted to pursue in order to improve profitability was streamlining their manufacturing operations globally. This meant harmonizing all critical purchases for goods and services they needed during the manufacturing process, which meant decreasing the amount of vendors. There was too much variability between different production sites globally in the equipment, machinery, spare parts, and maintenance partners they had to use. They iden-tified that fixing and maintaining a broad set of machinery in the different sites was too costly and slow. If they could have the same machines in all locations, they could standardize the maintenance and always have the right spare parts to minimize downtime. Their operations were so large that even minutes of stopped production would cost millions. With Martin's experience and his firm grip of their challenges, he was able to understand that this was a great opportu-nity, because they had done similar work with other customers, but on a smaller scale.

> The customer's operations were so large that even minutes of stopped production would mean millions in costs.

Since there were different machinery standards globally, Martin initially thought maybe the purchases would be split up globally between two or three vendors to match the local requirements and split the vendor risk. In this case it would make sense for Martin to focus on one region, where they were the strongest, and win over that part of the business. After further discussions with the prospect, Martin realized the full benefits they needed to achieve would only come from having one global partner and one contract. If he couldn't align with their strategy, then this was not something he should pursue. There were one or two competitors who could offer the customer what they needed.

Martin's company had only done regional contracts, but they had just made an acquisition that would make it possible to offer a global contract. Martin had to internally sell the idea and convince the management team to create their global contract capabilities ahead of schedule, which meant making some changes in how they operate internally across 30 countries.

From the beginning, Martin took a strategic approach by helping the customer holistically. He remained positive about the possibility of tailoring their portfolio to align perfectly with the prospect's strategic initiative and help them improve profitability. Martin and his engineers visited local facilities and interviewed countless people throughout the process. This was a very demanding time in his life as he spent hundreds of days on this deal. He understood the customer's pain-points, met the right people and was finally able to influence the exact specifications they used in the official RFP document sent to Martin and his competitors. All this work was well worth the effort because they ended up signing a five-year contract.

Lessons Learned

From the beginning, Martin understood and focused on the right strategic initiatives for the customer; he centered all of his work around this initiative. In the end, it won him a very profitable deal.

Notes

Chapter 11

Commercial Justification

Commercial Justification

Stakeholders can be more motivated to make a deal for a variety of reasons, including emotional involvement and a strong belief that the investment should be made, even if they've yet to calculate the return on their investment. Then, there are the stakeholders who are not as closely involved yet still need to give their approval for a deal to be made. These stakeholders require stronger justification(s) than those who are emotionally involved. A CFO or CEO will need a very compelling argument as to why the investment makes sense in order to agree; they often have competing ideas for what the money can be used for. That's why justification must be communicated through gains, as well as potential losses.

Financial Opportunity

What are the positive financial outcomes that the customer can achieve with your solution(s)?

Financial Risks

What are the immediate and future negative effects if they choose to do nothing?

What if they choose a different way forward? What are the risks?

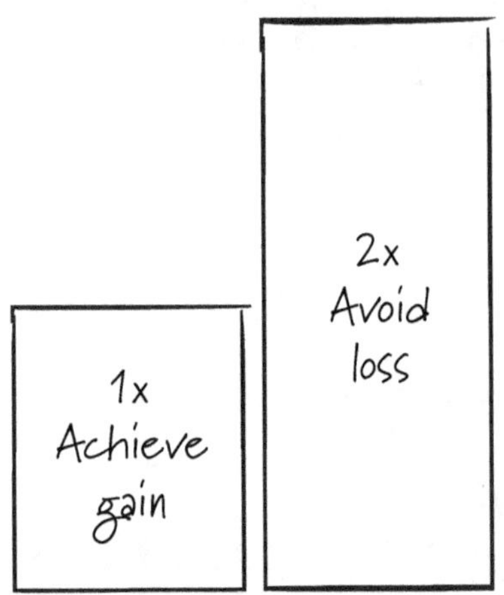

According to research (by Kahneman & Tversky 1979) people are twice as motivated by avoiding risk of loss, than achieving gains.

Building the Business Case

Having a realistic business case and trustworthy references are two important things that help position the solution for the decision-making team and C-Level.

Based on the information uncovered in the discovery phase, a realistic business case is often required.

Since the business case is based on numbers, each of the layers here needs to be described with numbers, not just words.

What are the customer's main business objectives and what financial targets are they looking to achieve?

What problems can/will stop the customer from reaching their objectives if not solved?

How much are their problems costing them now?

How much will their unsolved problems cost them in the future?

What are the key metrics that will be used to measure impact and progress?

What is the best solution to solve their problem(s)?

What are the different impact scenarios for the solution —worst case/average-case /best-case?

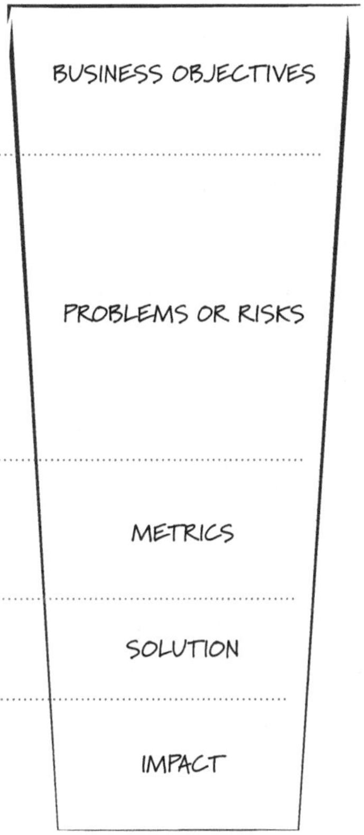

Simple Business Case Example

In many instances, the business case doesn't need to be extremely detailed. It just needs to be practical, easy to understand and based on realistic data provided by the customer. Sometimes, even a really simple value calculation can be good enough to justify a larger investment.

An IT-director and his team were in the process of buying new remote conference technology. "Jon," a seller of remote conference technology, had been talking to them for several months; his technology was a top candidate early on. After the customer's first evaluation round, they didn't want to talk to Jon any longer as they were already confident that they'd found the right solution for their needs.

> The loss of productivity was in the multiple millions on a monthly level.

Jon knew the company was making a mistake because this was a great fit based on the discovery meetings. Jon also knew the competitors he was up against. He didn't have anything to lose so decided to use a riskier approach. Jon got in touch with a stakeholder from the C-Level and was able to develop enough interest to get a meeting. Through this new stakeholder, Jon acquired an even better understanding of how the company used remote conferencing technology in their everyday business. This new stakeholder was frustrated, because in every online meeting they always had to spend several minutes in the beginning getting everything to work.

Based on how many minutes they currently spent in online meetings, and the average salary of the employees, Jon was able to calculate what their loss of employee productivity was at the moment. The loss was in the multi-millions on a monthly basis. The C-Level stakeholder ended up becoming his sponsor and strongly advised the IT team to change the priority of their requirements. A few technology specifications that were important to the IT-team were pushed aside and now user experience became the key priority.

A few months later, Jon's solution was chosen and implemented in over 50 countries. It was a risky move to approach new stakeholders, but in this case, it worked.

Lessons Learned
A simple calculation can often be good enough if it's based on numbers the customer has provided and is linked to a painful problem.

Notes

Calculating the Risks of Not Having a Solution

"George," a software account executive, was selling a new product that helped companies backup their IT-systems in real-time. He'd been in this new position for six months with little success so far in getting prospects interested. In his previous role, he was used to communicating the value of his solutions compared to the

customer's old solutions, but now he was selling something that was much less tangible. When he learned to communicate how customers were exposed to risks, he started having immediate success in the manufacturing industry.

> The calculations made it very clear, that it would make sense to invest.

He started asking questions like:

What if your production systems crashed, what would be the impact?

What if you couldn't get your systems back online right away, how much would that cost you per minute?

For each client, George made a simple risk calculation based on real-life cases of crashed production systems. He would then calculate the numbers together with clients to discern if it made sense to invest in a real-time back-up system. Such calculations make it very clear that investing makes sense. While in this role, George ended up saving hundreds of millions of dollars and a lot of headaches for many customers when their systems crashed.

Lessons Learned

Anything can be made easier through numbers. Numbers are not always necessarily precise, but even estimates help the customer make decisions. The value proposition should often be positioned differently depending on the unique pain points and metrics customers use in different industries. George found success with manufacturers, once he learned how to talk about the different manufacturing metrics and risks.

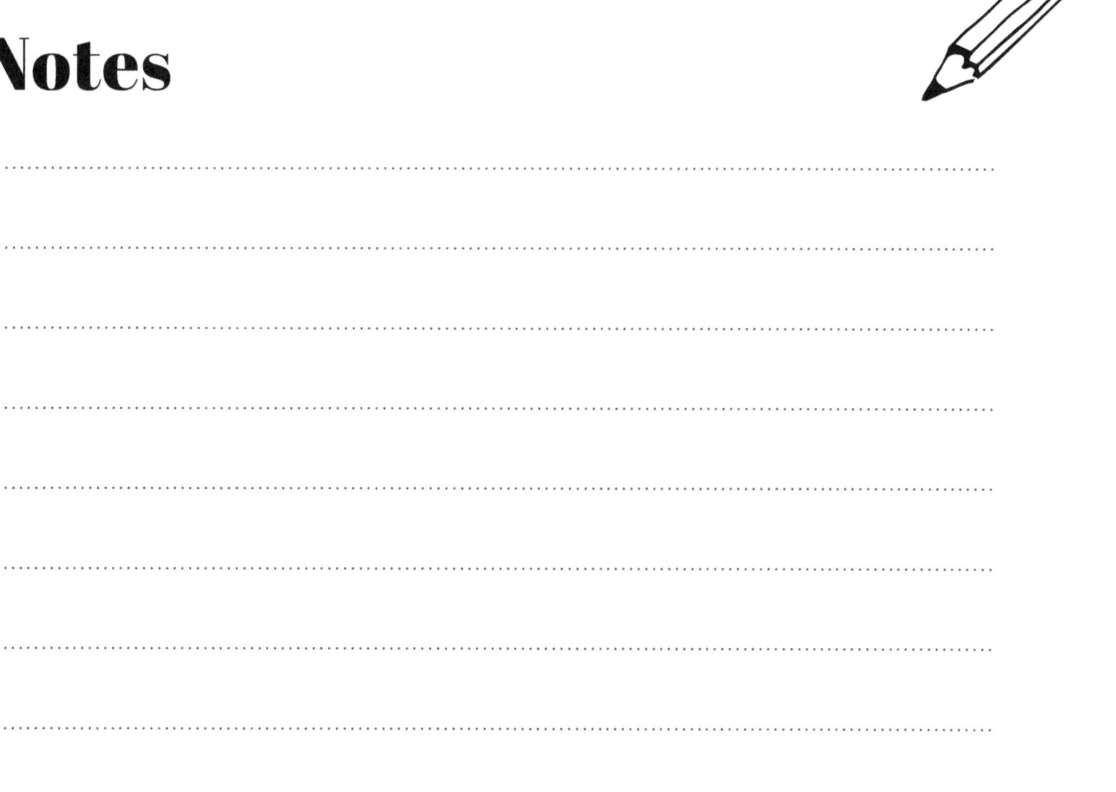

Notes

Notes

Chapter 12
Crafting the Proposal

Crafting a Winning Proposal

Here are some ideas for content that can be included in proposal presentations:

The content and how detailed it should be depends on whether the deal maker is presenting to stakeholders who haven't been involved earlier or known stakeholders deeply engaged in the discovery process. Different stakeholders will be interested in different things. An executive will not need to understand the technical details, and those on an operative level will be highly interested in how the product or service works for them.

The sample content displayed here ties together the most important elements that came out of the interviews in regard to presentations and proposals.

The demonstration can include showing the real product, or, it can be a visual representation of the solution, a video, maybe supported by a whiteboard exercise that helps with comprehension of how the solution makes their problems go away.

PROPOSAL CONTENT

1. Executive summary

2. Customer's goals and objectives

3. Customer's identified problems

4. Solution overview

5. Demonstration

6. Business case

7. References of similar customer cases and their results

8. Implementation plan

9. Next steps

Sample Solution Presentation Slides

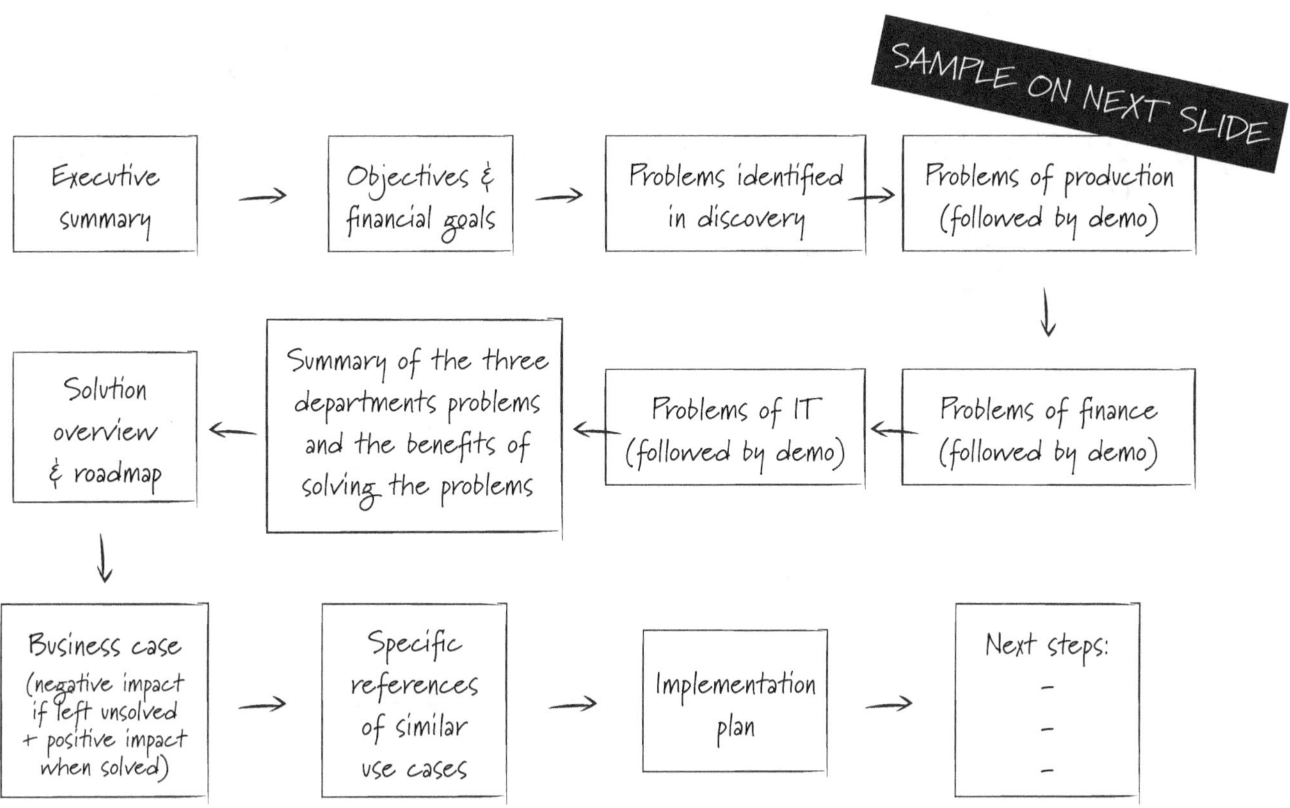

Production - Interview Findings

Jim Hoffman
VP of Production

Goals:

- Increase production capacity by 10% while keeping same cost structure

Challenges that need to be addressed:

- Lack of control and visibility of several production lines
- Unable to see real-time data of raw material purchases and material flow to production lines

Demo will show:

- Analytics: Analyzing different production line efficiencies
- Production Scheduling Module: Planning production capacity
- Inbound logistics module: Tracking raw material purchases

Start with the Customer and Work Your Way Toward a Solution!

"Jesse" and his pre-sales engineers held several discovery meetings with a customer and were now going to present their findings to the management team. The person who really wanted to buy their solution was one level below the management team; this was Jesse's champion. The champion was very advanced in her thinking, but the management team was conservative and not fully supportive of investing in new technology. Jesse's champion experienced some challenges communicating internally with the management team.

Jesse could be the needed help to get the management team on board. He knew he had to differentiate and excite, but recognized from experience that he couldn't do this with just his solutions and company, even though his company is considered a highly innovative organization. Jesse had to figure out a way to get the customer to first see themselves from a new perspective before addressing their challenges.

"This is exactly what I've been trying to articulate internally, thank you so much for finally saying what needed to be said!"

Jesse began his presentation about the customer's history with a focus on how they innovated through the years. He used pictures of legendary products they'd invented. He wanted them to remember who they are as a company! When presenting he asked them what products were in the pictures he showed them. He even memorized the years the products were first launched. He wanted to get to the heart and core of the customers DNA, which was innovating and inventing new products! From this he progressed to his companys story, what they are about and where they are going. He got them to see how these two companies are similar and share the same values for innovation. After this he moved to the normal presentation, that included the findings from the discoveries and how the challenges should be addressed.

The champion was extremely thankful afterwards. She approached Jesse later, saying, *"This is exactly what I've been trying to articulate internally. Thank you so much for finally saying what needed to be said!"*

The presentation became an emotional and engaging discussion, instead of fact-based approach. Jesse had many valuable discussions after the presentation and he connected with many of the stakeholders in the management team on a personal, not just a professional level. This was just one meeting, but it ended up being a crucial meeting for taking a step forward in winning the largest deal for his company in North America that year.

Lessons Learned

Make your presentations an emotional journey about the customer, not just a fact-based approach about what you can do for them.

Champion Enablement

You'll need to team up with your champion to navigate the deal and sell on your behalf internally. The presentation material you create together that your champion uses to communicate internally is called the "champion's sales deck." In the beginning of the buying process, the champion's sales deck is used by the champion to inspire and make everyone aware of the opportunities and challenges. At this point, it doesn't include details about solutions yet.

One good way of creating a champion's sales deck is by taking some of the deal maker's materials and placing them on the customer's own powerpoint templates. This will be easier to use internally than a vendor's slides. The idea is to enable the champion to sell internally about the challenges and their impacts, instead of directly selling them on the solution. Later in the buying process, the champion's deck will include the deal maker's solution(s) as the best option forward.

A champion's sales deck can be created at any point, but the proposal stage is especially important because the deal maker needs to get his/her message across in more places than they have time to be in. Additionally, deal makers do not have access to all meetings where the investment decision is discussed.

Notes

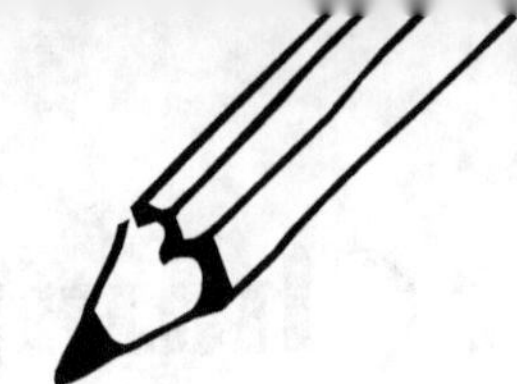

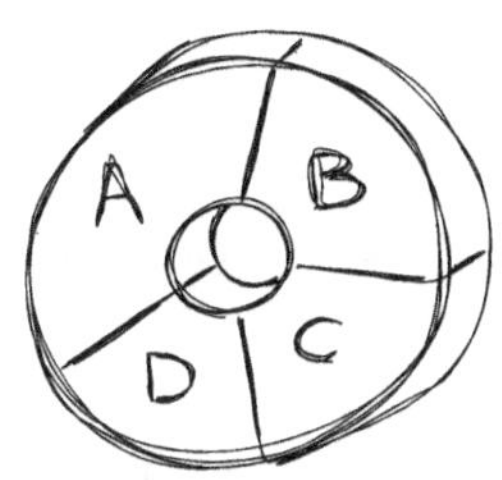

Chapter 13

Competitive Differentiation

Competitor Analysis

Knowing who you are competing against makes it easier to execute different types of offensive and defensive tactics that ensure you are positioned in the best possible way before negotiations.

Play with your strengths, aligning them to the major issues and needs of the customer. Deflect from your own weaknesses by bringing out the weaknesses of your competitors.

Examples of Strengths

- Proven track-record within solving similar clients problems
- Excellent remote support capabilities

Examples of a weaknesses

- Lack of local service
- Slower shipment delivery times

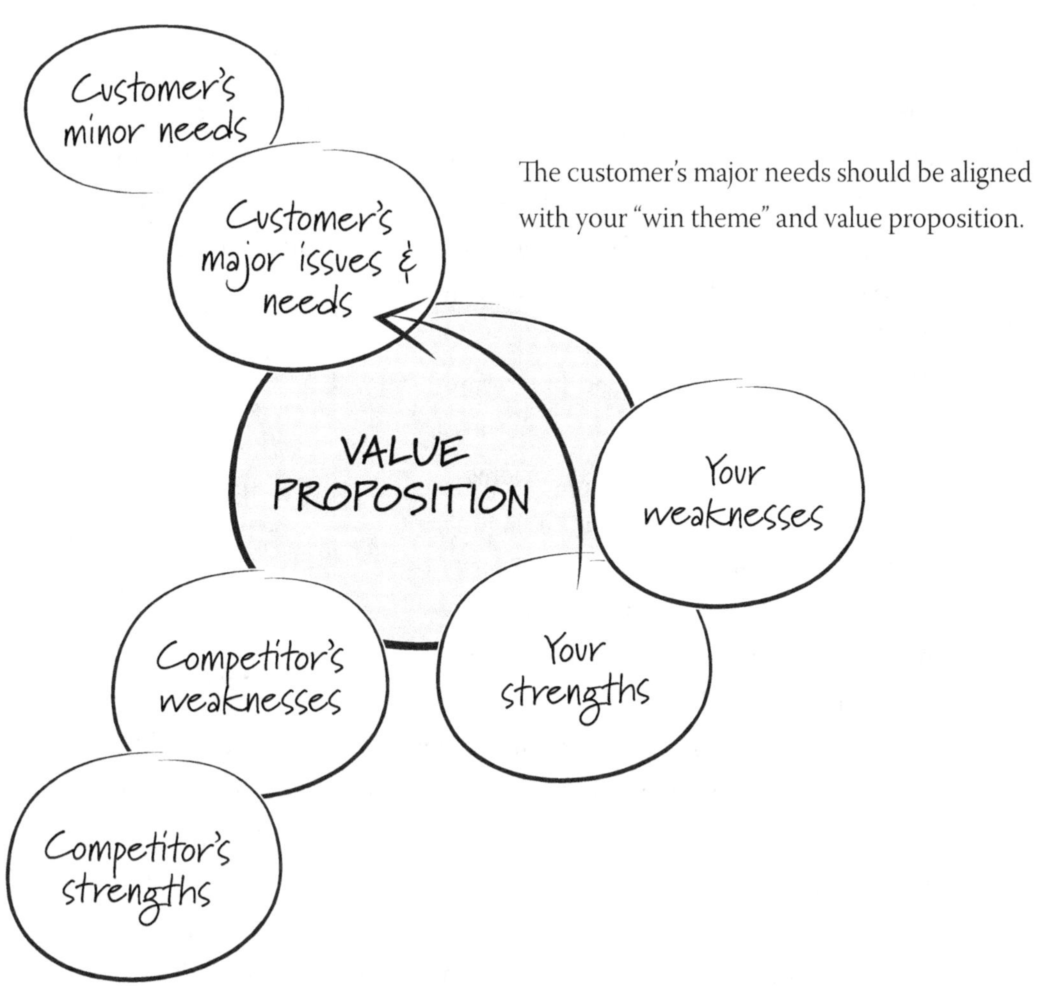

The customer's major needs should be aligned with your "win theme" and value proposition.

Leveraging Competitor Insights

About five companies were competing for the same deal. "Ryan," an account manager from one of the competing companies was working closely with the project team assigned to choosing the right vendor. He had been able to collaborate with the customer before any other vendors and had also found someone who could eventually become his champion.

The other vendors had become involved later. The cooperation had been good, but towards the end of the deadline to hand in a proposal, the project team leader stopped providing information about what was going on in the background. Ryan didn't know what was going on, but luckily his champion gave him tips. Those tips allowed Ryan to react.

The champion called Ryan on Friday before the Monday deadline to say that the buying committee was going to drop Ryan's company (there were only two vendors left at this point) due to a few issues they had with their earlier proposal. This champion was the key to being able to working diligently the weekend before the deadline in order to position their updated proposal against the main competitor. The champion hadn't directly told Ryan about his competitor, but Ryan knew his competitors well and was able to figure out who his main competition was.

> Without the extra head's up from the champion—combined with competitor insights—this deal would have been lost.

Ryan knew the competitor's weaknesses so he used this information to strike at his opponent by challenging the customer about the risks they'd expose themselves to by choosing Ryan's competitor. Ryan understood which of the customer's critical issues the competitor's weaknesses linked to and even had a few anecdotes to back up his point of view shared during a phone call. Ryan, to this day, doesn't know exactly what happened in the background during the next week, but rumors suggest that the customer brought these things up in a meeting, and didn't like how the other competing vendor handled the situation. Two weeks later, they began negotiating contract terms with Ryan's team and signed a multi-year contract.

Lessons Learned:

Without the extra head's up from the champion, combined with the competitor insights, this deal would have been lost. Positioning against competitors is very difficult if you do not know your competitors well.

Find a Way to be Different Than Other Vendors

"Mark," a strategic account executive, finally got his chance to win the first deal with a prospect he had been pursuing for several years. He was invited to present a proposal to the management team at their headquarters in New York City. He was going head-to-head against three of his main competitors. The office space had glass windows so Mark could see what his competition were presenting. He saw that their presentations were all very stereotypical and product centered, "We are this, this is what we can do for your and here are our prices." Or at least this is how he remembers it, because Mark was ready to truly surprise the customer and do something different.

> "I think you should put in your order for your Porsche."

Mark was the last in the boardroom to present to the leadership team. He gave an introduction of himself, and then started his presentation with a slide that summarized how he and his team understood the customer's challenges. What he showed wasn't a direct copy of the documentation the prospect had provided Mark, but rather, an analysis of the customer's challenges. After they had discussed the challenges, Mark shared insights about how similar clients were coping with the same challenges and how his company had managed to help them. They only briefly looked at the proposal of the actual solution.

Towards the end of the meeting instead of asking for the sale, Mark pulled out the CEO's biography, who was also in the meeting. He read out a couple of passages he had highlighted, including a whole paragraph that symbolized how this company's mission and values had been born, which also happened to be extremely important to Mark and his company. As Mark read, he made eye contact several times with the CEO. Mark promised the leadership team that any of his company's employees who worked with them would read the CEO's biography first. Mark positioned his company as an extension of the prospect's organization, instead of just another vendor.

The CEO, stood up, shook Mark's hand and said:
"Mr.Account Executive, I think you should put in your order
for your Porsche".

Mark (stuttered in surprise): "W-w-why"?

CEO: *"Because you've got our business!"*

The CEO then closed his notebook, walked out and left the others to set-up the next steps in order to move forward with the contract.

Lessons Learned
Getting creative can be well worth the time on the right deals. Surprises are good, but surprises that link you in a valuable way to the customer are better.

Big Plays

Some deal makers describe how being really creative outside the basic sales process is the only way to differentiate because competitors are doing the exact same things in their sales process. These creative approaches are referred to as "**Plays**" or "**Big Plays.**" They get the customer to do something with you that they will not do with someone else. It's a bigger investment of time and resources that cannot be done on every deal, but used on the really critical deals that you want to win. This could be a kind of special executive briefing, a reference visit or a visit to a production facility where the customer's products or services will be produced. In some cases a "Big Play" can also be a discovery workshop with a special twist. With the value-added approach many deal makers are able to gain the necessary additional trust and improve their relationships with key stakeholders in a critical part of the sales process.

Here are a few examples of big plays:

Targeted events or customized workshops for this specific customer	Visits to other customers (with a well-thought out agenda)	Visits to production sites or innovation/R&D centers

Notes

Getting Creative with Big Plays is an Artform

"Michael," a highly successful deal maker, explained how his team prepared for a prospect to visit their facilities. Towards the end of the sales process, they decided to invite the prospect to take a tour of their production facilities (located in a different country) for a whole day.

Their main competitors also had facilities in the same city, so he knew the prospect was likely going to visit the competitor's facilities during the trip. Michael's company had great connections in this city and his team made lots of preparations for the guests to make a positive impact. This allowed them to clearly differentiate themselves from their competitors.

> "The preparations were like a mission brief for a navy seal team!"

Several days before the prospect arrived, Michael's team was onsite preparing the facilities for the prospect to arrive. They prepped a detailed schedule of the visit that included who would present which local employees to the prospect, so they would know exactly who would be in charge of manufacturing their products once the collaboration was started.

In the lobby of the production facility, the prospect's logo was painted on the floor. They ensured the facilities were fully cleaned and the floors properly waxed. They even rented a billboard advertisement close to the hotel with the name of the service they would be negotiating about so the prospect's team would see it when they were transported from the hotel to the production facility.

They even made sure that guests felt welcome in the local hotel with the help of their connections. When guests arrived, they had gifts waiting on their pillows at the hotel. The gift was a new book that had to do with manufacturing strategy, which was the main topic of the visit. On top of the book, there was a greeting card from the managing director that welcomed guests to the country, wishing them a wonderful stay.

The way Michael described the preparations was that it felt like a mission brief for a navy seal team with all details of the people who would be there during the visit and a minute-by-minute schedule with tasks and responsibilities for each member of the team. After the visit, the negotiations started and four weeks later they had signed an agreement.

Lessons Learned

Even if you have a successful discovery and are able to position yourself perfectly, sometimes what you are selling is not differentiated enough from your closest competitors. A deal maker can greatly impact the buying experience with their own creativity and personality.

Using Your Management to Influence the C-Suite

"Thomas" had been working on an opportunity for half a year. He had created a business case and ensured that the solution was a fit for what the customer needed. The customer was using a competitor's solution that was okay, but the main stakeholder (or champion) that Thomas was working with was not satisfied with the value they were gaining from the current solution. The champion knew that in order to replace the current solution she would need the approval of her boss, who was a member of the management team and her boss would need the support of other management team members.

> The whiteboard exercise with the CEO and the executive briefing was a giant success!

Together with Thomas they created an executive workshop concept, and arranged that Thomas's company's CEO, Harry, would meet together with three members of their executive team. Harry was considered as a thought-leader in their industry, but still they had to position this carefully to get a half-days time from the busy members of the executive team. Potentially, the project could be transformative for them, and the business case was used to spark their interest. After some scheduling difficulties, they were able to find a time. Thomas, Harry and another colleague flew in to the prospect's headquarters to meet with the management team and a few other stakeholders.

The CIO was identified before the workshop as one of the biggest potential deal blockers. During a break in the executive workshop, the CIO and Harry did a whiteboarding exercise to go through how the platforms architecture works. The whiteboard exercise with the CIO and the executive briefing was a giant success and now the executive team finally saw what could be achieved and understood what the opportunity in front of them truly was. The CIO seemed much more neutral after this meeting and was happy to have had a chance to do the whiteboarding exercise with Harry. Half a year later, the contract was finally signed and implementation had begun.

Lessons Learned

Gaining access to higher levels is often possible with a strong champion. Gaining access to the C-level sometimes requires using your own C-level or other high-profile individuals as resources.

Notes

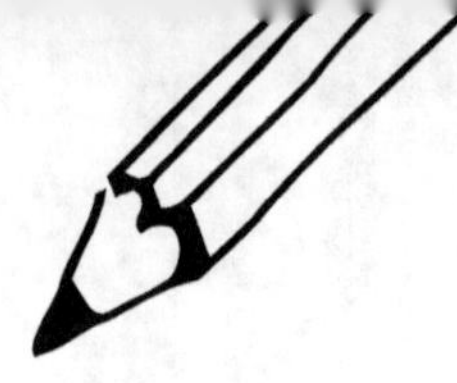

Chapter 14
RFPS

The Goal in the Customer Initiated Buying Process

When you haven't been involved earlier in the buying process and you receive an RFI or RFP, your goal is to take the customer back to discovery and "**re-frame**" the situation. This means getting the customer to reconsider what they actually need by re-evaluating something in the RFP that will add value to the customer.

One of the deal makers interviewed said he constantly sees flaws in the customers' RFPs, "Customers now do their own research and think they are experts, but they are in a rush and often don't have the needed experience to create high quality RFP's that are truly the best for them."

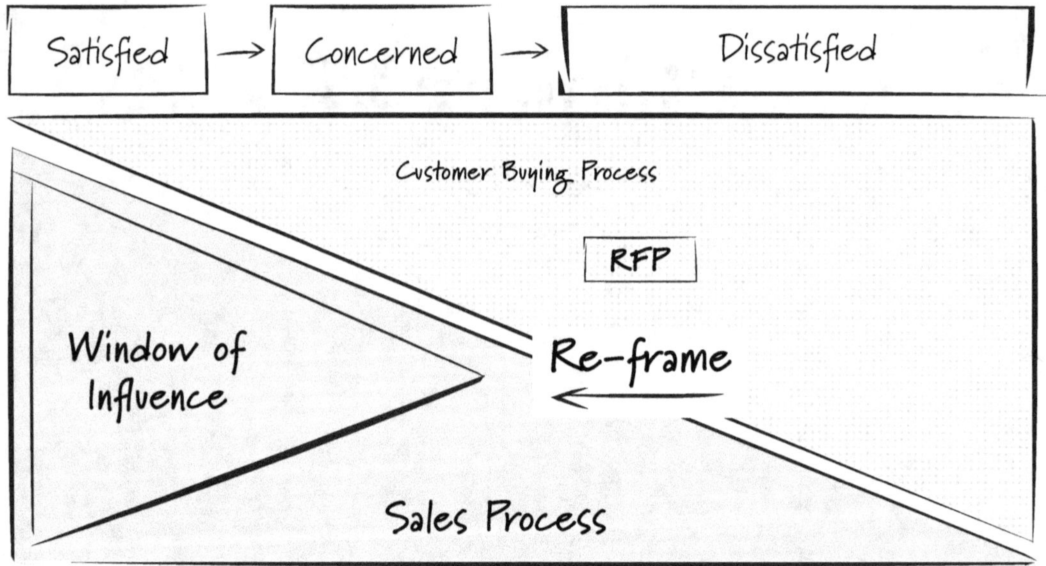

"When you receive an RFP that you have not been able to influence at all, think critically how you can differentiate yourself from your competitors. If you can't differentiate, spend time on something else."

The customer either does the analysis of their needs alone or together with someone, either way they have to go through a logical chain of thought to create the RFP.

If the deal maker is able to engage the customer in the Window of Influence, then they have a good chance to properly start at the top of this graph and work down to the requirements together with the customer.

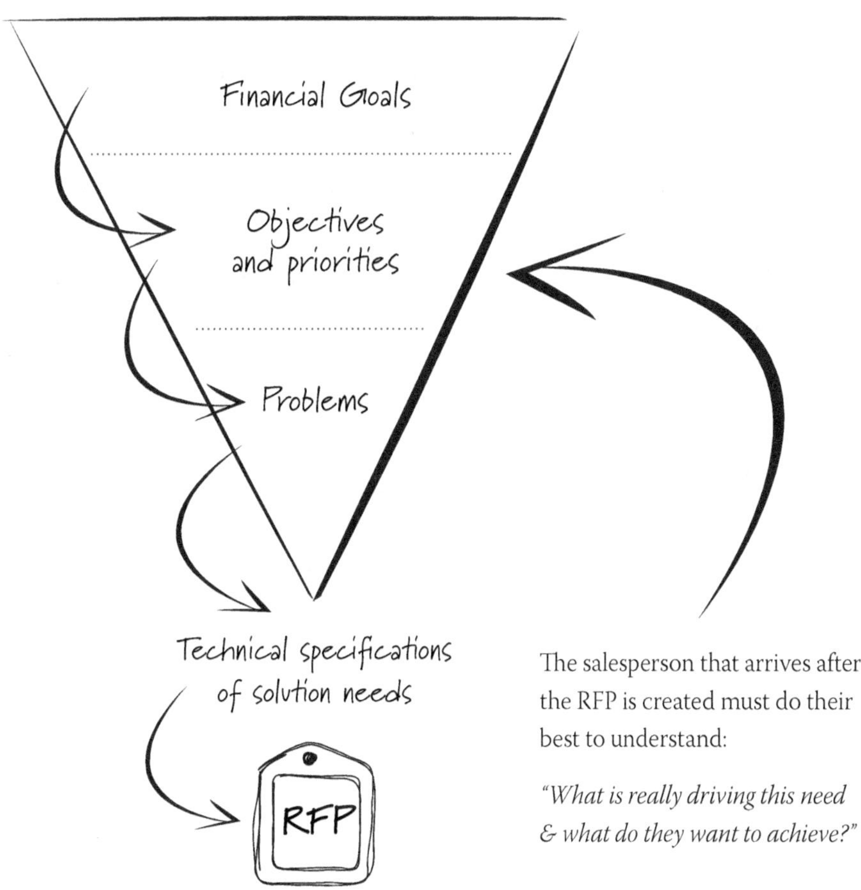

The salesperson that arrives after the RFP is created must do their best to understand:

"What is really driving this need & what do they want to achieve?"

If however the deal maker engages once the RFP has been sent, they have to work their way up and understand WHY the customer has certain specific needs. A deal maker cannot challenge the customer's requirements, without understanding the top of this funnel, but at this point customers are not often interested in discussing how they arrived at their specific requirements. When receiving the RFP, the deal maker often analyzes:

- Have they properly been able to diagnose what they need?
- Are they missing something important?
- Are they now locked in or flexible with the specification/requirements?

Not all RFP's are set-in stone and sometimes customers' are flexible about discussing alternative ways of solving their problems.

To Answer or Not to Answer an RFP

Nearly all of the interviewed deal makers will not answer an RFP if the customer is not willing to collaborate with them. This means if the customer sends an RFP and they do not want to meet and answer their questions.

Many of the interviewed deal makers actually don't bother working on RFP's that come as a surprise at all. Other deal makers critically approach them and qualify "hard" before deciding whether they should work on the opportunity or not.

"The customer often just wants to get a few proposals, because their internal policy requires a certain amount of proposals to be looked at before they can choose a vendor or renew their contract with the current vendor they are satisfied with."

"Random RFP's are often sent to us from prospects that just want a good price from us so they can pressure the other vendor that they really want to buy from."

"Randy," an account executive for an IT-service provider, received an RFP from an old customer that had switched over to their competitor three years ago.

There had been some issues with the service about four years ago, and that made switching over to the competitor an easier decision. Randy started in his current position a year ago and he knew the CIO from a past job, but hadn't talked to him in several years. Randy answered very politely that they won't be answering the RFP because his analysis told him that the competitor had a very strong foothold of the customer. The CIO called Randy during his summer vacation and almost begged him to reconsider. He was able to convince Randy that they did in fact have a good chance at winning the competitive bidding process. The CIO was very engaged and gave access to the information they needed. They put in a lot of work, but eventually lost the sale.

When they met with the CIO to get feedback on why they lost, the CIO explained that they realized they don't want big changes after all and that the other vendors pricing model fit their needs better.

Lessons Learned

Randy later learned that he had been taken advantage of because the CIO needed another vendor to participate in the bid in order to have enough vendors to compare (company procurement policy).

Challenge With a New Point of View

"Mike," a sales executive, received an RFP from a company he had never talked to earlier. This company had been working with a local vendor for 10 years. Mike was able to book a short phone discussion with the person responsible for the bidding process to try to understand why they would want to change vendors. The person wasn't able or didn't want to describe what the current vendor could be doing better, or if they were lacking capabilities in some area. The RFP was just a five page document, and one of the the worst that Mike had seen, because it lacked many important detailsthat are typically outlined in an RFP. It just included very high level descriptions of what they were looking for.

> With a 10 year relationship the current vendor had become lazy and wasn't up to date on the latest standards.

Mike wanted to meet the prospect because it was an interesting account with lots of potential. He knew he would have to challenge the prospect and change their point of view somehow just to get a meeting with them. He decided to not answer the RFP directly, but propose a completely different approach and only spend a couple hours creating the presentation. Typically Mike and his team spent many weeks working on proposals. They sent the proposal and the customer became so interested, that they invited Mike to meet with them and discuss further.

It was in the meetings that Mike was able to challenge the thinking of the customer and get them to see how much better things could be. With a 10 year relationship the current vendor had become lazy and wasn't up to date on the latest standards. With his differentiated approach Mike was able to eventually win a part of the business from this account.

Lessons Learned

When the odds are against you but the account is interesting, you can try a differentiated approach, than what the customer is asking for in the RFP.

Notes

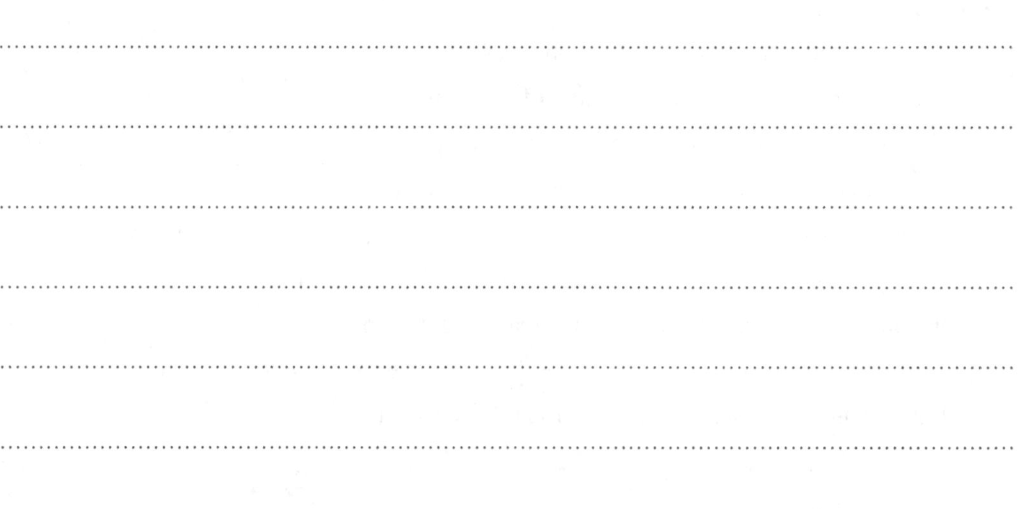

"Pat" received an RFP out of the blue. Based on the timing of the RFP, Pat knew they had very low chances of winning. She also knew that she would have to get one of her best experts to join the meeting to ask the tough questions from the customer.

When they met the customer, they presented on a high-level how they would approach solving the problems explained in the RFP. They had picked out some parts of the RFP and put them on slides. They asked the customer to explain how these different requirements were decided? The customer wasn't able to answer a few important questions. At this point the customer realized there were clear quality issues in how their own technical architects had built up the RFP.

> The customer realized there were clear quality issues in how their own technical architects had built up the RFP.

Two days after the meeting the prospect called Pat and asked them to visit again to look at the requirements.

Pat and her pre-sales expert were able to stall the buying process by several months and change the requirements. They gained the trust of the customer by finding the gaps and issues in their scope of requirements. This hard work paid off and they were able to win this deal that had a low probability to begin with.

Lessons Learned

Without changing the RFP or challenging parts of it, it may be a waste of time to participate in a bid.

Checklist for Surprise RFPs

Industry leaders and companies with great marketing can create lots of trust before a deal maker talks to the customer

Yes

1. Influence prior to receiving RFP

a. Have they been exposed to our content enough to give us an advantage? ☐

b. Has someone recommended us to them? ☐

2. Qualify FIT

a. Is this customer the right size for us? ☐

b. Do we want to sell to this vertical? ☐

c. Does our portfolio match with what they are looking for? ☐

d. Do we have suitable references? ☐

e. Can we differentiate from other options they will likely look at? ☐

3. Qualify relationships ☐

a. Do we have access or can we gain access to the right stakeholders?

Based on this information make a rational decision whether to pursue or politely disengage.

4. Willing to engage ☐

a. Are they willing to answer our questions? ☐

b. If we have valuable insights, will they listen to us?

Get the Prospect to Tell you Why You Should Answer

"Anton," a deal maker in his mid 30's had been working with one division of a large company. The other major division had always been working with a competitor and based on what Anton knew, they were very happy in the other division with his competitor. For the competitor, this was a strategic customer that they took very good care of. Anton had met them and knew the people in the other division, but had never done business together.

One day, the director from the other division called Anton and said they would start a new project and wanted Anton and his company to bid for the project. They would be sending the RFP in a few days. He was very skeptical about this, and thought there was a very high chance the customer would just use them to put pressure on the current vendor, keeping them "honest" with pricing.

"Are you serious about this or do you just want a different vendor's proposal to compare"

Anton did an internal evaluation of the potential project and the summary was that they had a very low chance of winning (Antons self-built qualification excel showed a 20% probability). Anton decided, that he would have one more discussion with the customer before deciding what to do.

In the meeting he challenged them and asked questions like, "Are you serious about this or do you just want a different vendor's proposal to compare?" He was able to get the director to sell them the idea of why they should bid for the project.

The director explained what areas they were experiencing challenges with, what they needed and what the situation with the current vendor was. After this extra meeting, Anton knew their chances of winning were much higher than he originally thought. They ended up winning the deal and still do business with both divisions today.

Lessons Learned

Without getting the customer to openly explain and "sell" his thoughts about why Antons company could be a good partner for them, it would have been very hard to evaluate what the chances of winning were.

Notes

Checklist

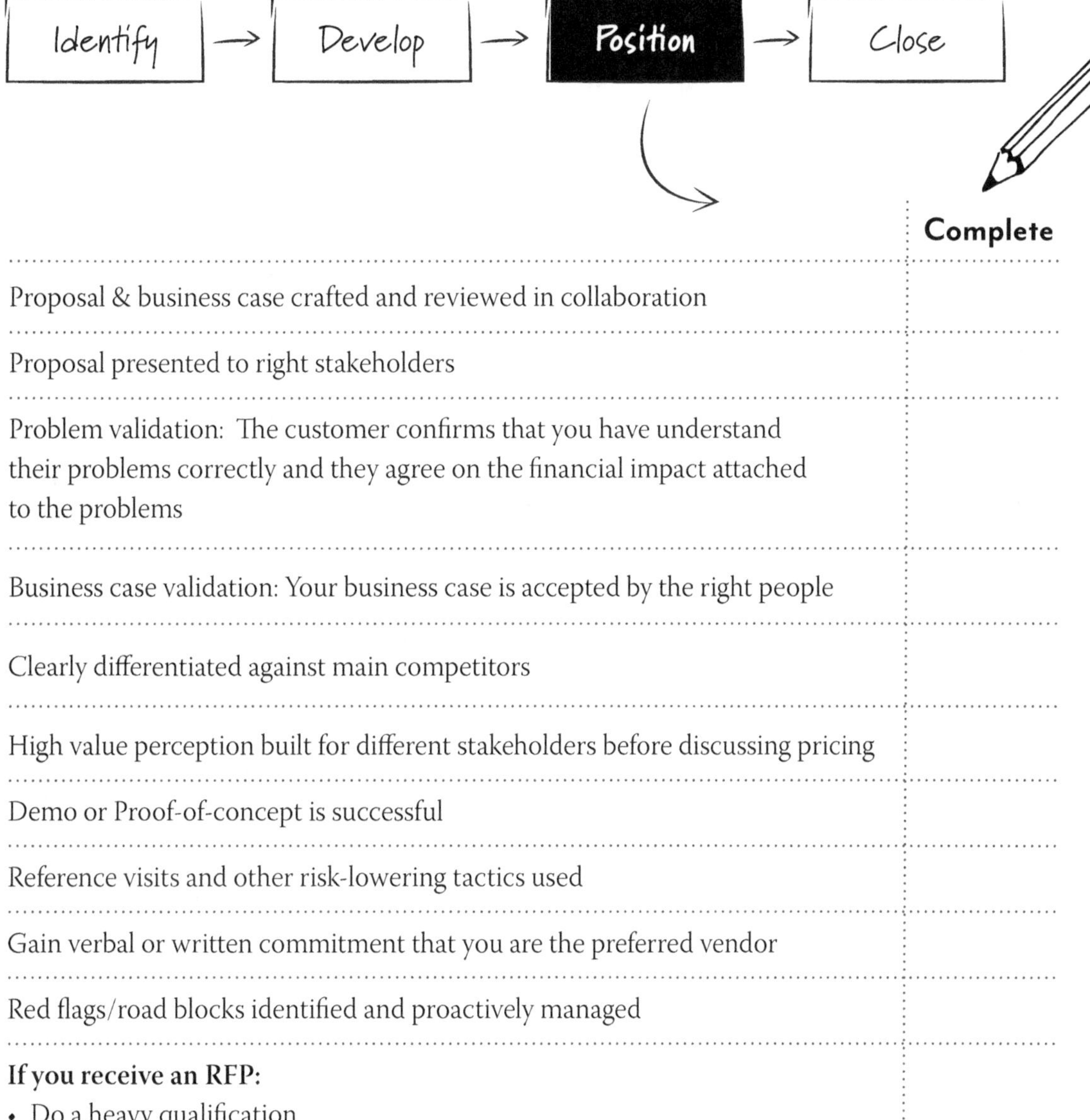

Proposal & business case crafted and reviewed in collaboration

Proposal presented to right stakeholders

Problem validation: The customer confirms that you have understand their problems correctly and they agree on the financial impact attached to the problems

Business case validation: Your business case is accepted by the right people

Clearly differentiated against main competitors

High value perception built for different stakeholders before discussing pricing

Demo or Proof-of-concept is successful

Reference visits and other risk-lowering tactics used

Gain verbal or written commitment that you are the preferred vendor

Red flags/road blocks identified and proactively managed

If you receive an RFP:
- Do a heavy qualification
- Re-frame to influence requirements and clearly differentiate
- Get customer to commit to discovery

Notes

PART IV

Close

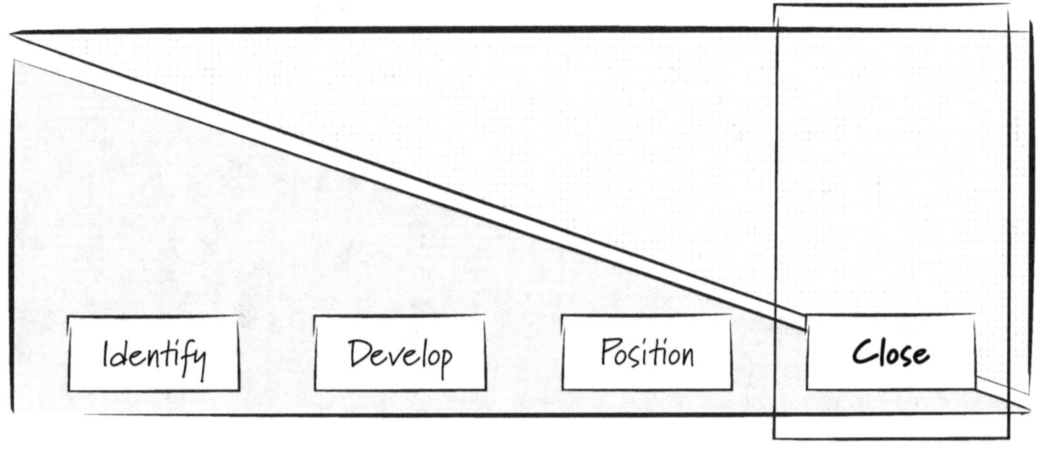

Goal of This Stage

Sign an agreement
as soon as possible

Minimize the
perception of risk

Keep your margins healthy in
the negotiation by leveraging
the value that your solution
will create

Smooth out any problems
without causing harm to your
relationships with stakeholders

Get good contracts terms

Speed up the decision process

Evaluate Your Deal Making Habits

Before negotiating, do you usually understand the official and unofficial purchasing process of the customer?

How do you react to the customer's discounting requests?

When you give the customer something of value in the negotiation what do you usually get in return?

How do you prepare to deal with procurement in advance?

How do you use your own superiors/management to assist in the negotiations?

Notes

Chapter 15

Preparing for Negotiations

Defining Negotiation

Negotiation by definition means:

"Discussion aimed at reaching an agreement."

In some cases, if you agree on pricing, terms and conditions, there is no need to negotiate; the objective of the deal maker should be to get the customer to sign the agreement immediately without any delay. Most often this is not the case because the customer knows they can reach a better deal by negotiating and putting up different competitor options against each other to squeeze out the best possible deal.

By the time the purchasing process for the customer has reached this stage, it is very rare that the different vendors are able to build up their value proposition or make their business case much stronger.

All value building typically happens before this stage. When a deal maker has done a good job building trust by cooperating & co-creating with key stakeholders in the Develop stage, and also positioned themselves properly, they will have a solid foundation to succeed in the negotiation stage.

The deal maker should as early as possible get written confirmation of different commitments from the customer, especially when the deal makers company becomes the preferred vendor. Verbal commitments are easy to back out of, so deal makers always need to get things in writing.

Examples of items included in negotiations:

- Contract length
- Products and extra services included
- Warranties
- Delivery terms
- Service-level agreement
- Price
- Payment terms
- Liabilities & fines
- Intellectual property rights

The Negotiation Game

Depending on the size of the agreement and the industry, you may just have one or two negotiation rounds to adjust the contents and pricing before the customer commits to signing the agreement.

The goal of the deal maker is to keep the price, as high as possible and the terms as good as long as they can, while the customers negotiating team has the opposite goal. If you give concessions early in the process you won't have any cards left to play with. Professional buyers and procurement will attempt to get sellers to commit to concessions of longer payment terms and price discounts as early as possible when they know that vendors are hungry to stay in the game. Later they will keep pressuring and have more demands. Experienced deal makers know how customer's negotiate and will prepare for the customer's typical tactics in advance to keep their negotiation position as strong as possible.

Examples of typical steps in the negotiation of a complex deal

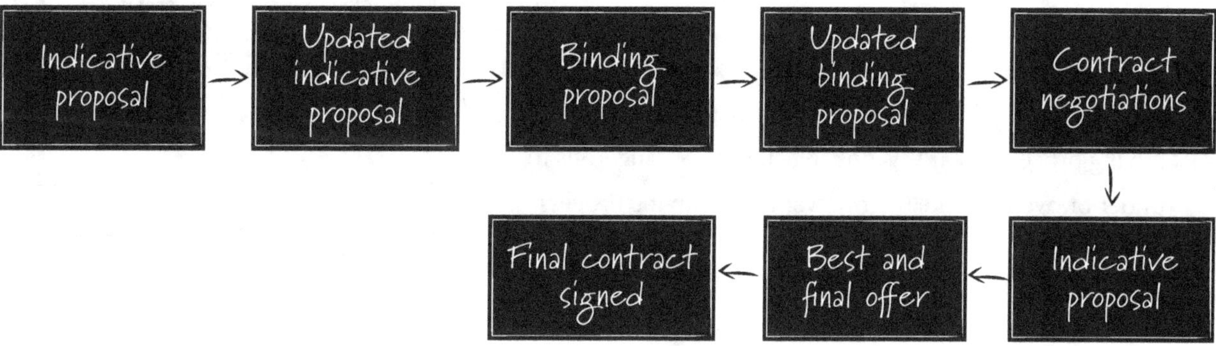

The Role of Procurement

Procurement professionals are becoming more and more common. Procurement is often even involved in very small deals. Their role is to get the best possible deal for their employer. A few of the interviewed deal makers told stories of how they have been attacked on a personal level by procurement managers in an attempt to pressure the deal maker to giving discounts.

As a deal maker, it's critical to understand that the role and guidelines of procurement varies from company to company. When working on a deal and procurement is involved, it makes sense to at least analyze the following:

- Are they just managing the purchasing process or do they have the power to make the final decision?

- Can they block or persuade buyers to choose a certain solution?

It's important to identify the role of procurement in the buying process as early as possible. It can be dangerous to under or overestimate their power in the buying process.

Examples of tasks that procurement are responsible for:

- Assist in vendor selection

- Create buying criteria and rank potential vendors

- Create RFI and RFP/RFQ documentation

- Pre-select a short-list of vendors for the business decision-makers to continue discussions with

- Negotiate final agreements, terms and conditions

- Manage the list of approved vendors

Working with Procurement

**Here are some comments and tips from deal makers about working
with procurement:**

A procurement process can drag on forever because of minor issues. Procurement needs to get a win for them before they allow the deal to proceed. Something as small as a few grand discount in a multi-million deal will matter to them. They are not in a rush and are patient until they get their discount.

Sometimes subscription services between 0-200.000 per year can go under the radar without having to be passed through an official purchasing process, especially if the purchase doesn't need to be presented to the management and board.

If the investment needs to be presented to the management and board they will always want to know what the other options are, so be ready to compete and deal with procurement even if you haven't been aware of other competitors being involved.

Procurement typically causes some type of crisis at the last stages of the negotiation to try to get concessions. This is especially true at the end of a quarter or at the end of a year, as they know the vendor will be more likely to want to get the deal closed.

A trusted relationship built with the right people will help you navigate through the negotiations with procurement.

If you know procurement will be involved at the end, it's a good idea to leave a bit for them to chew off on the price to make them look good, so they can win.

Always discuss in terms of money, not in percentages.

Small concessions must be done with procurement, otherwise they won't let you through. he key is to prepare for this in advance, and keep your cards close to you and hidden until the end.

Notes

Working with Procurement

"Mark" had been engaged with a prospect for over a half a year, regarding an IT-infrastructure investment they would make in order to launch a new commercial application. Marks hard work paid off. They were told they were the preferred vendor. At this point the business area president requested procurement to close the deal. Before procurement stepped in, they had already agreed on a high-level pricing model.

The prospect had a very complex and bureaucratic procurement process. They were notorious for having an army of legal people involved when contracts were created. At this point there was only three weeks left until the end of the fiscal year. If this deal slipped into the next year it would mean a loss of commissions around $80,000 for Mark. For Mark, this would be a big boost to his salary.

> The disagreements didn't have anything to do with price.

Their next meeting was onsite at the prospect's premises. A few managers from procurement, two representatives from the business area, and a lawyer were sitting in the meeting room. Mark asked how fast they could create the contract and at this point the lawyer said, they cannot sign a contract before they have the frame agreement accepted. At this point the lawyer noted that they had never created a frame agreement with anyone in less than 6 months. This was a huge personal problem for Mark, because he needed to close this within three weeks to get the full commission.

This was even a bigger problem for the customer, because they had already communicated to their customers about the launch of their new application but they didn't have the required infrastructure in place yet.

Mark asked, *"Is this impossible or could we in theory get this done in three weeks?"*

The lawyer, said *"no, it's not impossible".*

Mark: *"Ok, if it's not impossible. What needs to happen? "*

Together with procurement and the lawyers, they went through why it typically takes so long to create a frame agreement. Mark found out that it usually takes a long time to get frame agreements done, because the agreement gets sent back and forth between the two parties. Small changes can take several days to get answers, and it requires the feedback of several different people from both sides. This was the problem so they came up with an idea to expedite the process. Mark proposed that they book a cabin for two days, and negotiate all the parts of the frame agreement together onsite. Both parties key personnel went to a cabin for two days to do the work. Not everything was solved in the frame agreement during the two days, but all important concerns were at least brought forward so that they could be handled much quicker. It turned out that the disagreements didn't have anything to do with price related issues. The major conflicts had to do with IPR-rights and liability issues. By the end of the two days there was around three deal breakers from the customer's side that needed to be solved, otherwise the deal would not go through. Marks company had a very big interest in winning this deal as it would be one of the biggest deals of the year for them so they had a team of people solving the problem and they were able to find resolutions to these issues.

9 PM on the last day of the fiscal year, the agreement was signed.

Lessons Learned

In retrospect, Mark realized that without the procurement managers cooperation and drive, this deal would never have happened. The procurement manager arranged all the necessary internal meetings and authorizations in record time and also made the two day cabin workshop possible. Many other things in their schedule were re-scheduled and this deal was prioritized by the procurement manager. Mark learned that procurement can even become a champion at the end of the sales process. This case is also a good example that shows how contract terms and legal details can often be much more important than price. This deal taught Mark that even very difficult challenges on a tight schedule can be overcome when both parties want to find solutions.

Notes

Price is Just One Part of the Equation!

Only 8% of B2B buyers choose the vendor who has the best price.[1]

Price often plays a much smaller role in the customer's decision-making requirements than they are willing to admit. The risk of project delays and poor results of the implementation have larger potential costs associated than the difference in vendor pricing usually will.

Successful projects often lead to promotions and successful career advancements, while poor decisions sometimes lead to people being fired.

In larger decisions, there are typically several people whose careers and reputations are on the line. If projects fail, so do they.

The more complex a decision is, the larger of an impact it has. Big-impact decisions are not always rational as a result. According to deal makers, it's the decision-makers and other stakeholders personal perceptions of value and risk that bear greater weight than price.

Price is Just One Part of the Equation

A deal maker's comment about the role of price in one deal:

"I had been working on a deal for about a half a year when we started negotiating. I knew they were looking at a few other options. A person on the buyers team that I had developed a good relationship with stated in an unofficial discussion that they are willing to pay 15% to 20% more for what we were selling, because they see us as the premium option. More than that they wouldn't be able to accept as a price premium. They believed that working with us would minimize the chances of failure and they trusted we would deliver what we promised. Our price was not far off from "where it needed to be" and with a few minor tweaks, we were able to sign an agreement. I think we were able to get a great price for this deal because we were able to engage this customer very early. We were able to properly position our value to them in a very clear and compelling way."

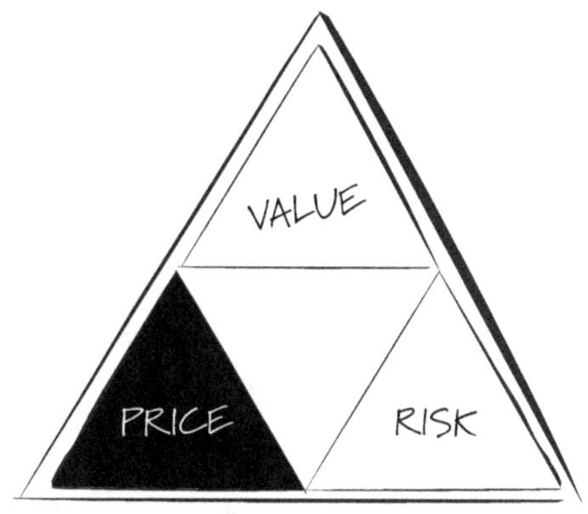

Risk is More Important Than Price

Deal makers explained how decreasing the feeling of risk for the customer was crucial to winning deals. Research supports their point of view, too.

The graph on the right shows how risk is the buyer's lowest concern early in the buying process, but then it becomes the most important concern when a decision is being made.

In the early buying stage, it's the customer's needs and solution options that play the most important role. When the customer has good options to choose from, and want to make a decision, their focus shifts to the risks and cost of the different options. If a deal maker needs to start building the perception of the solutions value when it's time for the customer to start making decisions, then it's too late.

Even though customers' don't necessarily think about risk as the most important thing earlier in the sales process, its something the deal maker can influence from the very first steps of the sales process by behaving and operating as the most trustworthy vendor. Most of the things covered in this book, when done right, will position you as the high value, low risk option.

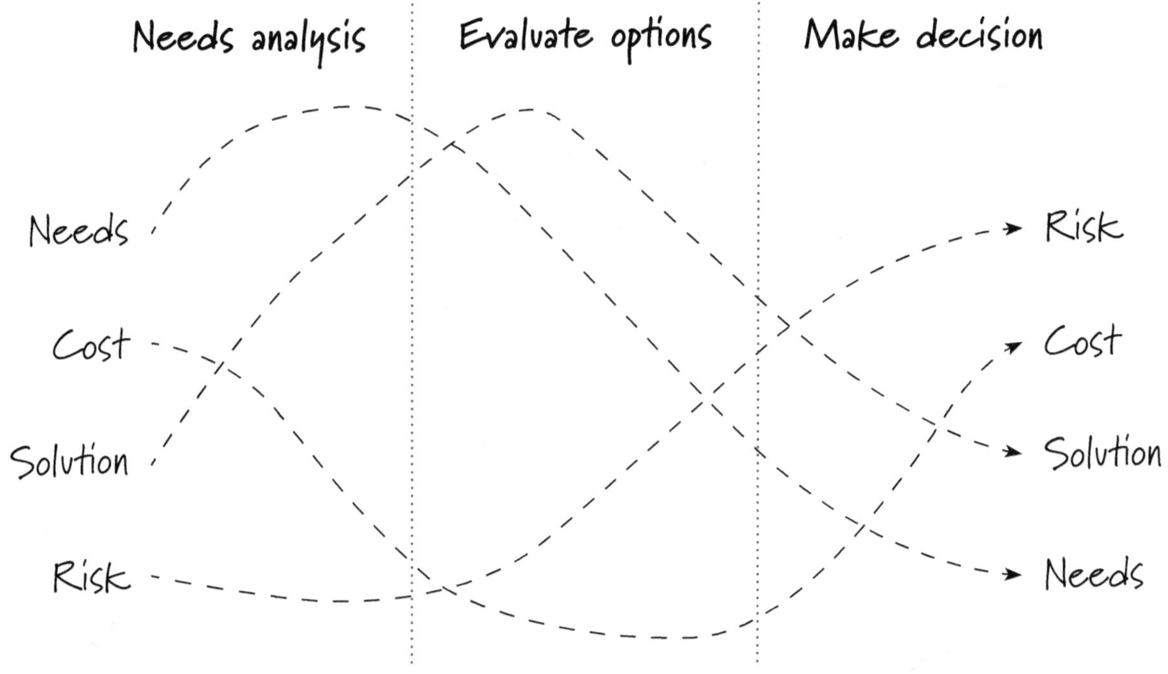

Original research by Neil Rackham. Mentioned for example in his book,
Major Account Sales Strategy.

Deal Makers Pre-negotiation Preparation Tips

Analyze:

- Which stakeholders are on the customers negotiation team?

- What are their personal goals and agendas for this deal?

- What are they looking to gain from the negotiation?

- Which stakeholders are still against us, who is neutral and who is on our side?

- What are their other options? (Direct and indirect competition)

- Are we in a unique position or is our solution easily comparable to competitors?

- Are we the preferred vendor? If yes, what is our evidence of this?

Notes

....

....

....

....

....

Close Plan

The better your relationship is with your main contact or champion, the easier it will be to create a realistic close plan.

When the customer is ready to move into the negotiation phase, even if you are the preferred vendor there are many things that can still go wrong and there can be major delays that slow down the deal that you may not be aware of.

In order to keep the momentum up and avoid misunderstandings, it helps to proactively identify the remaining barriers to closing.

The goal of a close plan is to understand the customers approval process by writing down all remaining tasks that need to happen up until the last step which is signing the contract and starting the implementation or delivery.

The close plan is typically done together with the champion and should include as much detail as possible. Details might include whether the contract will be signed electronically or on printed paper and where and who will be present in the meetings where approvals are needed.

Sample Close Plan

Date	Task
Oct 21	Deadline for updated proposal
Oct 22	Updated proposal approved by VP of production Jim
Oct 24	Contract review with procurement
Oct 28	Final contract review and authorization from CFO
Nov 5	Signature from CEO
Jan 5	Implementation started

Notes

Chapter 16

Designing the Win-Win Situation

Partner or Opponent?

The deal maker's goal when negotiating is always to achieve a **win-win!**

Closing a deal isn't about the deal maker "winning," it's about both parties feeling like they got the best possible outcome in as smooth of a way as possible.

It's not the best way to start a new partnership if the other party feels like they were pressured or tricked into making a decision.

The deal maker should always focus on maximizing the value of the agreement so that both parties feel like they've won.

Negotiations are all about mindset and psychology. In order to maximize value for both parties a partnership mindset has to be adopted. It is always good to remember that it's the customer's responsibility to get the best deal they possibly can and that it's nothing personal if someone on the customer's side challenges or attacks you in any way.

In some situations, if there is a risk that the negotiations will get unpleasant it makes sense to leverage others within the organization so that the deal maker doesn't risk hurting his/her relationships with the stakeholders involved.

Maintaining an Open Dialogue

At this point, the deal maker should have earned the ability to have an open dialogue (at least with the champion or sponsor) about what needs to happen in order to win. Many deal makers recommend asking the right stakeholders in the end of the sales process questions like:

> *"What still needs to happen in order for us to sign this agreement"?*

If you have an open and trusting relationship you have a very good chance at getting the customer to say exactly what still stands in the way of signing an agreement. If they don't want you to win at this point, they may leave things unsaid or even lead you in the wrong direction.

When you ask to move forward, and the customer says they cannot, most deal makers do the following:

- Understand what the reasons are for why they are not ready
- Ask, "What if x or y were taken care of?" and then they see if the customer would be willing to move forward if these issues were handled
- If the customer's requests are truly the only concern(s) that stand in the way of signing the agreement, then you can go ahead and see what can be done on your side without making any promises

Since it's the customer's duty to get the best possible deal for their company, they may often request unreasonable things that they don't even expect to receive.

Using Small Trade-offs Can Have a Big Impact

What If?

Small trade-offs can have a big impact. Being creative and flexible is the key. Without promising, explore what could be a resolution to the objections that the customer has. The goal is to never give something of value, without gaining something valuable in return. Get commitments and decisions in writing.

To explore alternatives, use words such as:

What if we….?   Imagine if we could…?   If we helped with…?

Notes

....

....

....

....

....

....

....

Things you can give or receive of value:

Give to customer

- Faster project delivery (expedite resource use for customer)

- Extra training or additional training packages

- Additional products free of charge (limited time)

- Innovation center visit for project members

- Free process audit

- Senior consultants named to project

- Premium support package

Receive from customer

- Longer contract period

- Shorter payment terms

- Reference permission

- Testimonial

- Delay project start to a later time (when you have more resources available)

- Frame agreement to cover other product areas

Small Trade-offs Matter

An insurance company was going to make the type of technology investment that would require a portion of their workforce to be re-trained. If the training failed, it would expose them to great risks, which could mean thousands of unhappy employees and a major loss of productivity. "Mike," a senior sales manager working for a technology vendor, was one of their three options. One way that Mike was differentiated from the competitors, was his company's change management model and training solutions. The customer's team really liked the ide of having one of the vendors deliver and take responsibility for the training, but later they said that the price of this would be too high and that they would take care of the training with their internal resources.

> "What if the training is paid for by us, would that make you want to sign the agreement."

To Mike, the training was after all just a small part of the deal, because they had a very efficient training concept that included online training modules and remote training. If the prospect wanted to take care of the training, that was fine by Mike, but he knew it might turn out to be a critical issue later. Because of this Mike decided in his internal calculations to leave the training costs into the scope of the budget he was proposing. This way, it could later be removed if negotiations got tough and he could still maintain a healthy profit for the deal.

Once the scope of what Mike was offering was locked, and price negotiations had been going on for a while, it was looking like they were going to win the deal. One night, Mike received a call from the leader of the prospect's project team, and the message was clear: headquarters had not been willing to sign the agreement. They had told the project manager that the price was ridiculous and no where close to where they could come to terms. Something needed to be done or they would hand the deal over to their competitor who was still actively involved.

Mike sensed that this was just the typical drama that buyers pull in the late stages of negotiations so he played along and said this was the final offer. He assured the prospect that he doesn't believe there is anything that can be done anymore, but he will check with his own superiors. The next day, Mike called the project manager and said he had been working all day to figure out what could be done. He asked, "what if the training is paid for by us, would that make you want to sign the agreement?" He knew the project leader was worried about them having to take care of the training on their own. The project leader called their headquarters about the latest developments of getting the vendor to pay for the training. To HQ he positioned this as a big win for them.

HQ was satisfied with this and they signed the new agreement. Both parties were happy with the outcome.

Lessons Learned

This approach would not have worked if Mike hadn't built the value of the training in the beginning. This is a good lesson to never give anything for free, as it can be used later in the negotiations for leverage.

Leveraging Your Management in the Final Stages

"Hanna," an account director at a small service company had been working hard for three years to get a new customer. Her competitor was ten-times bigger and had a proven track record. As a small player, Hanna's company could potentially be a risk for the customer if their resource capacity or know-how was not enough. This competitive situation was a real David and Goliath story.

In order to show the customer how important they were, Hanna was able to get her company's CEO to commit to a few things in the final stages of negotiations:

The first was that the CEO promised he would personally be onsite for a day in their production facility to get to know their business.

> The competitors CEO would have never done the same.

Second, the CEO gave his personal number to key people on the customer's side in case anything went wrong or they ever wanted to have a chat with him. That created a personal touch and gave a personal promise to always be available for them.

This extra effort was needed to differentiate themselves from the bigger competitor whose CEO would never have done the same. In addition to the CEO's commitments, they had a clear roadmap of development items. They were not just a service vendor, but an active partner developing the business. That's how they won the deal.

Lessons Learned
Choosing Hanna's company was a riskier move, but the prospect saw them as a business development partner who was more committed to them than the other vendors.

"In one deal that I was working on and ended up winning, one of the keys to victory was not the slides and materials I was using the with the customer. The most important slides were the ones I used to communicate internally with our management team to keep them updated. Having them help me was crucial for winning the deal and gaining the needed trust from the prospect. Once or twice a month I would send a report to them of the status and progress of the opportunity. This way when I needed their support they knew exactly what the situation was and they were happy to help. The whole point was that I kept them in the loop before I needed them so I never needed to brief them when we were in a hurry to influence the customers key decision-makers. My approach got our management more invested in this deal, and I'm sure they invested more time into this than they usually do."

The quote above explains how one of the interviewed deal makers ensures his company's management team is willing to help him win big opportunities, by using their influence to engage with the customer's management team and other stakeholders high in the customer's hierarchy.

Small Things Matter

If you are even with the competitor, as is sometimes the case, then the deal can swing either way depending on who's more focused and proactively finding solutions to the customer's objections.

When competing companies have been working on a deal for months or even years, the difference of value between the vendors that the customer perceives can be quite small. Both competitors have developed relationships with the customer. Both have solutions that fit the criteria, but who will the customer choose if all else is equal? When all else is equal it's the small things that define who wins and loses.

If you've been able to clearly position yourself as the more valuable (or lower risk option), than it will be much easier in the end. Then again, it's not in the customer's interest to reveal that a vendor is in a strong position to win, and will therefore often keep it a secret as long as they can.

Even small concessions in the last days and hours of negotiating can be the difference, when all else is equal.

A manufacturing company wanted to buy a simple solution to improve the efficiency of their warehouse.

When "Martin," the account executive, started talking to them, he was able to discover that their challenges weren't as simple as they thought, and what they were trying to achieve in the next few years would require a much more innovative approach. What the customer needed was business-critical and a simple solution was not adequate. Martin knew their competitors would offer exactly what the prospect was asking for, but if Martin could get the customer to look at their situation differently, then the competitors would have a hard time matching what Martin could offer.

A "courtesy discount" was enough to get the customer to sign.

After several meetings with Martin & his team, the customer's technical advisors started asking more detailed questions as they became more aware of their problems and how they should be solved. Together, they started working on a plan. They were also working with competitors but the way his team was able to educate and position their concept made the negotiations much easier.

From Martin's first proposal, the final price ended up being around 0.5% less. Martin's manager helped him close this deal and said the price discount in the end was irrelevant because the first proposal was already positioned high. The manager called it a "courtesy discount."

Lessons Learned

Even though their proposal was priced significantly higher than their competition, a minor discount was enough because Martin's solution was unique.

Notes

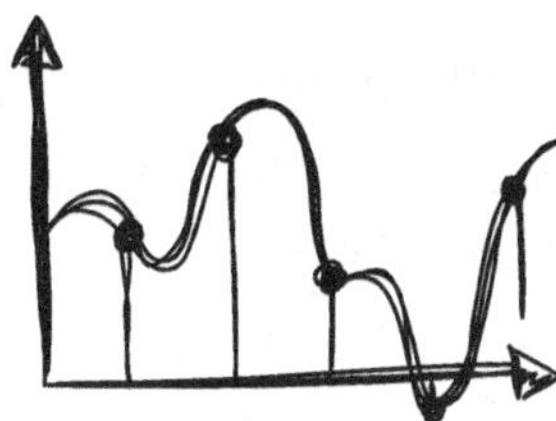

Chapter 17

Keep the Momentum Going

Focusing Until You Close

"Oscar," an account director had been working on a deal for over a year. The final decision would be made on a Monday morning in a board meeting.

Oscar knew that they were on par with their main competitor. The deal structures of the two vendors were similar. The technology was quite similar, too. And the service organizations were on par. From the customer's point of view, either decision would be workable. Oscar made sure he would be available all weekend if the customer had any last minute concerns. He also made sure that his direct superior was available in case he needed approval for something. The final proposal had been handed over to the customer earlier that week, but Oscar still had the whole team available in the event any changes were needed.

> In the final stretches of the negotiations, all else being equal, the one who wants to win more has a better chance of winning.

On Sunday night, a call came in from the customer's CEO at 9.33 PM. The board members had held a pre-board meeting dinner and decided that they still wanted a better deal. They needed something more from them. Oscar knew they would make the same call to his competitor.

Oscar called his superior, who was in his garage working on his car, but was expecting a possible call that night about the deal. They decided to make a few minor changes in the final proposal related to the pricing model and the service package.

On Monday morning, the CEO called Oscar to let him know he had won this deal. Oscar heard weeks after the deal had closed that the competitor's key account director had also been called on Sunday night, but wasn't able to get in touch with his superiors that night, so he couldn't modify his proposal in any way.

Lessons Learned
In the final stretches of the negotiations, all else being equal, the one who wants to win more has a better chance of winning.

Notes

Cooperating Consistently Until You Close

Eight vendors received an RFI from a utilities company that was looking for a new partner to help operate their multiple facilities.

"Morgan," an account director received the RFI, but he wasn't sure whether they should participate at all. He didn't have any suitable references and no previous business relationship, but he knew that they did have a differentiated approach from other competitors that might fit nicely with this prospects situation. All the signals were saying

> "It's going to feel weird now that you are not calling me every friday afternoon"

that this was a very low probability case due to their lack of relationship with the customer. Maybe, just maybe, if they would have engaged with this company before they received the RFI they could have immensely increased their chances of positioning themself as their #1 choice from the beginning. They answered the RFI, and after that there was five vendors left that got the RFP and Morgans company was one of those that received it. At this point he started building his opportunity team, which consisted of several experts from a few different teams.

From the start, Morgan's opportunity team was able to cooperate smoothly with the customer. Every new version of a proposal that they created, they created together with the customer and their different project team members.

They were able to build relationships with most of the customers project team and Morgan was able to build a close relationship with the CPO (Chief Procurement Officer). Everytime before they sent any new material or updated proposals they always verified the changes with the customers project team, and Morgan verified them separately one-on-one with the CPO. This was key to building a strong and trusting relationship.

Morgan called to inform the CPO every single week on Friday afternoon between 4-5 PM, to let him know about their progress. He held these calls to keep the CPO updated on progress and issues, and also ensure they were on the right track. If there was anything that Morgan felt should be modified, he and his team would stay as late on Friday nights as needed in order to update materials for the prospect by Monday. Toward the end, most Saturdays and Sundays were spent at the office as well. Morgan's team was never late with deadlines during the competitive bidding process. One by one, competitors were eliminated until one Friday afternoon, during their weekly call, the CPO told Morgan that they would like to proceed with Morgan's company. The whole sales process from receiving the RFI to signing was 9 months.

In the signing ceremony, the CPO told Morgan, "It's going to feel weird now that you are not calling me every friday afternoon." Morgan and the CPO still stay in touch and consider each other friends today.

Lessons Learned

Consistent cooperation and professional project management during the competitive bidding process can by itself already be a differentiating factor. Maximizing how much you co-create together can significantly impact the level of trust & proposal quality.

Fight Until the Deal is Signed

Time Kills Deals

In nearly all the analyses of won deals, the deal maker was able to proactively move the deal forward with proper intensity, ensuring momentum. When the customer says they are doing things internally to move the deal forward, they may not be completely honest. The deal maker should always know the details of what's happening on the customer's side in order to react to challenges.

In the won deals, deal makers knew the details of what was happening in the background. In lost deals, there were things going on that the deal maker didn't know about. Lack of transparency and collaboration in the end can slow down deals, potentially killing them.

Focus Until the End

Even when you have a letter of intent or especially if you only have a verbal commitment from the customer, your goal in the negotiations is to keep the momentum going until the agreement is signed.

Once the agreement is signed, start all implementation activities right away, because there is always a chance that deals can be canceled. Once the project has started the odds of stopping are diminished. One deal maker called this "throwing down cement," which should be done right away.

Regarding the paperwork, one of those interviewed said, "Work isn't finished until the paperwork is done." It may not be your favorite part of closing a deal, but it's still integral to your success.

"Johan" had been the sole vendor of a specific technology for a teleoperator for some time. The teleoperator sold this technology forward to their own corporate customers. One day Johan heard that the teleoperator had decided to change to another vendor with new technology that was yet unproven.

Johan explained the situation to his superior, "Francis," who was the country manager. Francis immediately booked a meeting with the customer's VP of technology. Francis knew the VP had to be challenged in order to get them to reconsider. This was important because switching to the other vendor could potentially harm their business. Francis challenged the VP:

"What would happen to your business if your strategic corporate customers switch over to you competitor because of this change? Do they trust you because you sell the technology or is it actually our brand name and reputation that is helping you get success with large corporate customers?"

> The new vendor had already celebrated the victory at their office, but they soon received the awkward call that the customer had changed their mind.

They spent a majority of the meeting discussing the risk of losing customers and what the reasons were for wanting to switch over to the competitor. The teleoperator had already verbally told the new vendor that they were the chosen partner and decided on the next steps in writing, including the date and place where the contract would be signed.

In the meeting, the VP had written down everything Francis said, and immediately after the meeting, called the people below him to get more information about why they had decided to change vendors. Two days later, Francis and Johan met with stakeholders below the VP, as well as the VP, and were able to sort things out.

The new vendor had already started celebrating their victory until they received the awkward call that the customer had changed their mind. Never celebrate until AFTER the contract is signed!

Lessons Learned

It's not over until the paperwork is signed and the work is started

If it looks like you are going to lose the deal, don't give up. Challenge the customer. Stakeholders higher in the organization may not be aware of the whole situation. Use your management to influence higher ups as needed.

Checklist

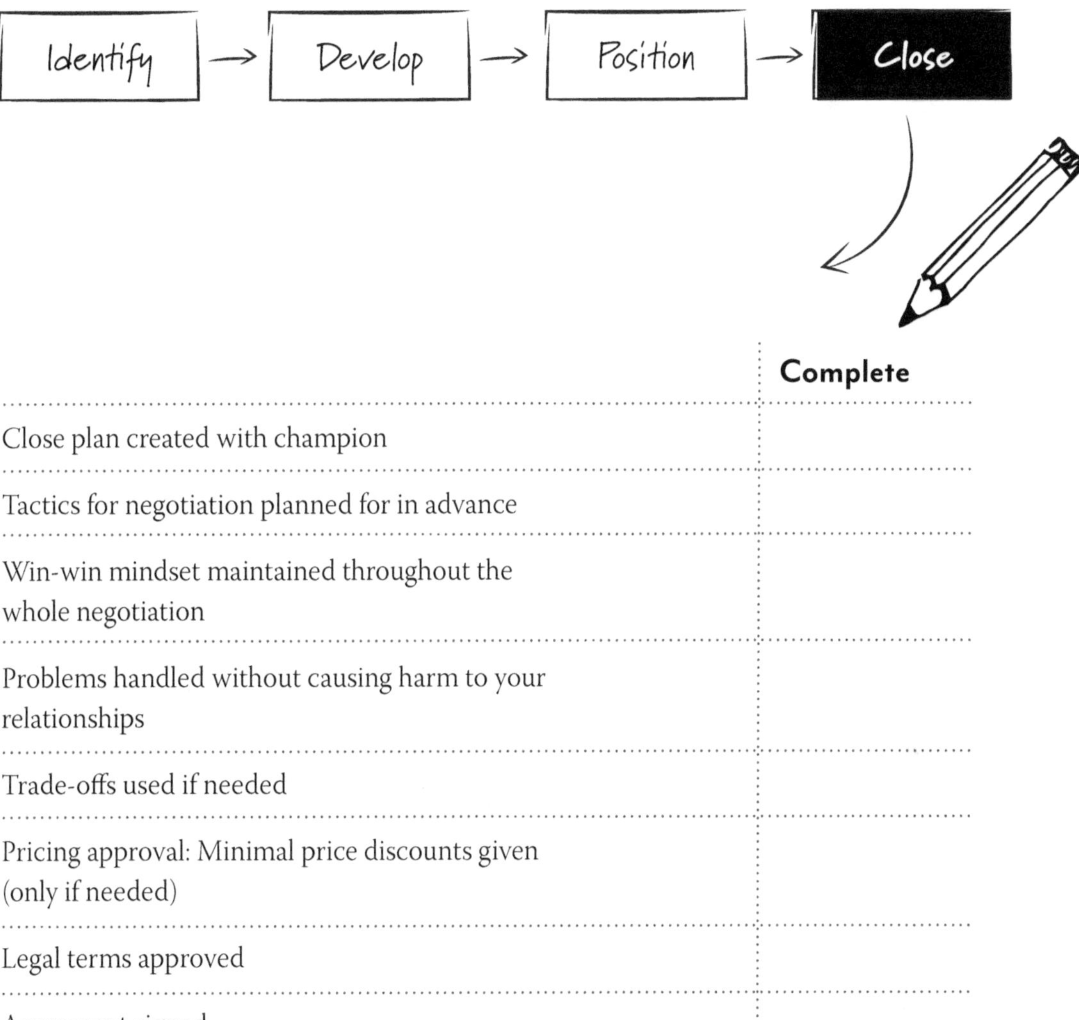

	Complete
Close plan created with champion	
Tactics for negotiation planned for in advance	
Win-win mindset maintained throughout the whole negotiation	
Problems handled without causing harm to your relationships	
Trade-offs used if needed	
Pricing approval: Minimal price discounts given (only if needed)	
Legal terms approved	
Agreement signed	

Notes

Deal Checklist & Deal Milestones

Deal Checklist

List of all key points from each sales stage

Deal Milestones

Major steps that must be taken to win a deal

Deal Checklist

IDENTIFY

	Complete
Meeting booked with the right stakeholders	
Challenges uncovered that are worth solving	
Pain validated by customer	
Potential champion identified	
Customer commits to explore possibilities further	
The opportunity is qualified (on both leads and sales person initiated opportunities)	
Opportunity plan created (if you decide to pursue)	
Mutual preliminary timeline created	

DEVELOP

	Complete
Champion found	
Champion helps gain access to key stakeholders & influencers (including executive sponsor)	
Business value discovery completed: You have diagnosed the customers needs and you have the necessary information to position yourself to win	
Technical discovery completed	
Measurable business pain is found and admitted by stakeholders in positions of power	
Win theme identified	
Heavy qualification complete (value, relationships, timeline, funding)	
Champion wants to buy and cooperate with you	
Mutual action plan created with champion	

POSITION

	Complete
Proposal & business case crafted and reviewed in collaboration	
Proposal presented to right stakeholders	
Problem validation: The customer confirms that you have understand their problems correctly and they agree on the financial impact attached to the problems	
Business case validation: Your business case is accepted by the right people	
Clearly differentiated against main competitors	
High value perception built for different stakeholders before discussing pricing	
Demo or Proof-of-concept is successful	
Reference visits and other risk-lowering tactics used	
Gain verbal or written commitment that you are the preferred vendor	
Red flags/road blocks identified and proactively managed before the negotiation stage	

If you receive an RFP
- Do a heavy qualification
- Re-frame to influence requirements and clearly differentiate
- Get customer to commit to discovery

CLOSE

	Complete
Close plan created with champion	
Tactics for negotiation planned for in advance	
Win-win mindset maintained throughout the whole negotiation	
Problems handled without causing harm to your relationships	
Trade-offs used if needed	
Pricing approval: Minimal price discounts given (only if needed)	
Legal terms approved	
Agreement signed	

Deal Milestones

IDENTIFY

Engage the
right stakeholder(s)

Identify business
critical problems
or opportunities

Gain commitment
to do discovery

DEVELOP

Engage and develop
relationships with stakeholders
in powerful positions

Discovery:
Uncover information &
educate the customer

- Strategic goals
- Objectives
- Challenges
- Needs
- Case for change

POSITION

Co-create a
winning proposal

Present and get all relevant
stakeholders on your side

Ensure the full value you
will create is understood
before negotiating

CLOSE

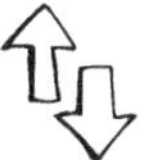

Fight to keep profit
margins healthy

Keep legal terms &
conditions favorable

Sign contract

Deal Winning Principles

1. Always prospect & get involved early

2. Create value in every interaction

3. Think buying first, selling second

4. Get to power as fast as possible

5. Always find your real champion, not just a coach

6. Collaborate, don't push

7. Find the compelling reasons to buy

8. Leverage your own organizations resources and win as a team

9. Be paranoid about red flags that can stop your deals

10. Avoid pricing discussions, before the full perception of value is clear for the customer

Analyze your own deals that you are working on at the moment:

- How many of these principles are you applying on the deals you are working on right now?

- How many of these principles are a habit for you?

Notes

Final Words

At this point it's been a few months since I completed the content of this book. The journey has been long. First, it took me over a half a year to find the top-performers that would qualify for this research before I interviewed them. All in all, it took almost two years from start to finish. Lots of frameworks and concepts were created, and the best of these were chosen to be shared in this book, so I hope you can use them to help hone your own sales process. To support and validate the interviews and stories, I later decided to add in research data from other sources alongside my findings to better support your learning journey.

Now, it's time to summarize into just a few paragraphs what I believe to be the true secret to winning versus losing deals:

It's clear that the interviewed deal makers have an official sales process that they follow, but how they execute the process compared to less successful colleagues is very different. In the losses analyzed in this research, there was clearly less creativity at play. Smaller deals can be won with less creativity, but the more complex ones always require creativity. When we really boil down the major differences between won and lost deals, success seems to be determined by how creative and flexible the deal maker can be. Being a successful deal maker requires mastering the combination of creativity and extremely focused execution.

At this point you might still be wondering why *Secrets of Sales Innovators* was chosen as the title. This idea didn't actually come from me, but from my dear friend, Matt Lockwood (UK). The more I thought about it, the more the word "Innovator" made sense. An innovator, by definition, is "a person who introduces new methods, ideas, or products."

Each customer situation a deal maker works on is unique and, therefore, every deal that is won requires new methods and ideas. The ultra-competitive and complex deal stories covered in this book display incredible creativity from the deal makers to adjust their approaches. Deal makers have to consistently come up with new ways to help customers in order to drive deals forward, often in ways not taught in traditional sales training and certainly not formally documented.

Determination, drive, focus, hunger, the will to win, ruthless execution are qualities that everyone I interviewed possess. But when it comes to winning those deals, it's about repeat innovation on each and every deal. Crazy ideas and big plays mentioned in this book are displays of innovation and creativity. The way deal makers co-create, collaborate and develop value for customers is a highly innovative process. Ruthless execution + deal specific innovation = Success in complex deal making.

Come to think of it, sales professionals don't get enough credit for their everyday innovations as they work on extremely complex opportunities. To sum up: If you want to win big deals you must be a sales innovator!

Hopefully, you were inspired by this book to be a better #salesinnovator and a true difference-maker to your customers.

If you enjoyed this book, please take a few minutes to review it on Amazon or GoodReads, as well as sharing your thoughts on social media. Feel free to email me your comments or reach out on social media. I'd love to hear your thoughts or feedback!

Resources

For free resources like templates and articles about winning complex deals, visit the website:

www.SecretsofSalesInnovators.com

About the Author

Jan Ropponen's mission is to make salespeople more valuable to their customers and help make a positive impact on society. The more value salespeople create during the sales process, the better they perform.

After a successful sales career, Jan now focuses on helping B2B sales teams grow in highly competitive markets. He works with companies from industries such as telecom, manufacturing, insurance and technology. Jan advises and trains both sales management and sales executives on topics such as modern sales methodologies and opportunity management.

Contact Jan for speaking, consulting or training inquiries:
jan@janropponen.com
+358 50 5169392

Acknowledgements

"Don't make friends who are comfortable to be with. Make friends who will force
you to lever yourself up."
– Thomas J. Watson

There must have been nearly one hundred people who have in one way or another
contributed to this project. Many have become friends through the process and that must
be the best part of this project. I've made new friends who share a passion for educating
the mind and improving the state of the wonderful profession of sales.

Thanks to the team who made this project possible:

Rebecca Housel, thank you for your patience and showing me what professional book production is
all about.

Mikko Johansson, thank you for your fantastically creative ideas that made my drawings come alive.

Paul McNamara, thanks for pushing me and opening up my eyes to the wonderful world of
publishing.

Thank you to the people who have most closely mentored me throughout this project
Jouni Varpelaide, Mika Riekkola and Matthew Lockwood.

Thank you to all of you who helped give feedback in the early stages of this book. This book would
not have been the same without you.

Thank you to all those Sales Professionals who were interviewed for this research. What you do is
nothing short of amazing and this world would not be the same without your stamina and desire
for continued excellence.

Appendix

Research Background

I was sitting with the VP of service and an account executive from a technology vendor that I was collaborating with at the time. We were jointly selling state of the art software. The account executive spent a lot of time talking about the solution and the demo. He did a bit of discovery but it almost seemed like he didn't think going deeper into the customer's situation would be beneficial. He told me several times, "Let's just see if they like our solution." He talked about the solution and how some customers see its value and others wouldn't.

At the same time, I was working with one of his colleagues. Even before a first call with a customer this other colleague researched the industry and had insights to share. He wanted to understand what the customer's business strategy, goals and pain points were. He really wanted to comprehend what needed to happen from there for the customer to reach those targets. He understood that his solution could provide immense value, but only in certain situations. He had to uncover the problems and understand their root causes.

These two account executives both had the same technology, backgrounds, manager-support, training and pre-sales resources. Everything the same on the surface, but the results: night and day. One of them was kicking-ass while the other had to find another place to work after some time for not achieving adequate results.

I kept noticing the same differences between sales people in other companies. They had the same sales process, but their approach to executing it was different. How they focused on certain parts of the sales process was different, too.

This observation and the countless discussions with sales leaders and sales pros about best practices of deal making lead me to making the decision to do this research to study the best deal makers. I wanted them to answer tough questions and make them reflect on what has truly made them successful.

What I Wanted to Better Understand

The main question that I set out to find the answer to was:

What are the best practices that unite successful sales professionals that consistently win deals between 100.000€ and 10 million?

Everything presented in this book is based on the findings from the interviews of over 30 top performers and the analysis of over 100 deals (both won and lost).

The primary focus of the deals analyzed were in situations where new innovations were sold to existing customers or selling to entirely new customers.

The goal was to make the findings highly valuable for anyone selling larger solutions, regardless of whether they focus more on new or existing customers.

Backgrounds of the Interviewed Sales Professionals

The sales professionals interviewed are top performers in their sales organizations, many of which are international companies. Most are either the best or among the best globally. They get consecutive invites year after year to their companies Presidents Clubs and receive other awards for their exceptional performance.

The companies they have worked for or currently work are top leading companies from industries such as ICT, manufacturing, professional services and outsourcing. Six out of ten of the largest software companies in the world are represented by those interviewed.

They are from countries such as such as The United States, Mexico, Italy, Germany, Spain, UK, Finland, and the Netherlands.

Many of those I've interviewed have been promoted to sales leaders and many are also executives these days, so some of the insights and lessons they shared are also through their experiences from deals, their team members have won or lost.

Many of those interviewed do not want any recognition for their success, but wanted to share their teachings and remain anonymous. For protecting the privacy of the individuals and the competitive insights of their employers, the names in the stories were changed.

Typically, deal sizes of the persons interviewed was between 100k-10M€. 25% of those interviewed have also won on deals over between 10M€, and 15% have won deals over 100M€. What became clear through the interviews is that there can be just as much or even more complexity in a 200k software deal as in a 50 million capital investment deal, such as machinery.

Both their successes and failures have been analyzed from over 500 years of total experience. When estimating the total deals they've been involved in winning, its over 10 billions. That's a lot more than any one person can in a lifetime have gained experience in.

All interviews were done face-to-face or remotely. There was a total of 34 sales professionals that were interviewed, and many of the sales professionals were interviewed several times.

Respondent Profile

Experience

19.8 years of sales experience on average. (10 year minimum experience set for the study)

Estimated total deal value

The estimated total deal value these sales people have personally contributed to was over 10 billion. What raised this up was the fact that several interviewed sales professionals had also during their careers won large deals valued between 100 million and 1 billion.

Geographic area

26% have worked their whole careers in the nordics

41% have sold in multiple continents

32% have sold in Northern America

Industry

38% have sold software for a majority of their careers. The rest were quite evenly distributed between, IT-services & outsourcing, Manufacturing, IT consulting / Professional services and Telecom.

Differences in sales approaches

Some interviewed sales people approached new customers with a "land and expand" or "seed and grow" strategy, while others sold solutions that required the customer to make a larger investment from the beginning.

Channel vs. direct sales model

Many of those interviewed sold through OEM's or channel partners.

During the interviews it became clear that the same principles apply whether you are selling with channel partners or directly.

Notes

Chapter 3

1 - https://go.forrester.com/blogs/14-01-27-to_win_against_increasing_competition_equip_your_salespeople_with_a_deeper_understanding_of_your_buy/

2 - https://www.rfpio.com/blog/rfp-responses-answer-library/

Chapter 4

1 - https://www.challengerinc.com/blog/more-b2b-decision-makers-want-in

2 - Sales Benchmark Index 2013 (www.salesbenchmarkindex.com)

Chapter 7

1- https://www.challengerinc.com/blog/more-b2b-decision-makers-want-in

2 - https://www.gartner.com/smarterwithgartner/what-sales-should-know-about-b2b-buyers-in-2019/

Chapter 9

1 - 2017 B2B BUYER'S SURVEY REPORT (Demand Gen)

2 - https://www.slideshare.net/SAVO_Group/07-sirius-decisions-sales-enablement-market-and-trends-survey-revealedsiriusdecisions

Chapter 15

1 - SiriusDecisions 2015 (https://www.siriusdecisions.com/blog/pricenotthemostimportantdriverofbtobbuyingdecisions)